A REPORT ON THE FIRST FORTY Y
THE LONDON & NORTH WESTERN RAI

CONTENTS

INTRODUCTION

I seem to have the slightly dubious honour of being the longest serving active 'officer' of the Society, having served continuously since 1973 in the various capacities of committee member, Chairman, President, and Vice-President. I also have the lowest active membership number – 3. Oh dear, that really does make me feel suddenly old! Inevitably, I suppose, this has led to the task of bringing together, and editing, this 40th Anniversary celebration publication falling to me.

As with all such things there have been frustrations and difficulties, but on the whole the work has been interesting and stimulating. I have particularly enjoyed renewing memories of some of our wonderful past members, and indeed I have learned a lot of new things about them in the process of putting the notes together! As a lapsed modeller, it has been interesting to see what some of our members produce when not at Society events, whilst reading through hundreds of old publications, newsletters, meeting minutes etc., has reminded me of a lot of things I had forgotten about. How have all those years gone by so quickly?

Works like this cannot be put together single-handedly and a large number of people have provided valuable direct input for which I am very grateful. Their names appear with the material they contributed. In addition, I would like to record my thanks to those who provided help, encouragement and advice during the preparation work, in providing information and in reviewing material and helping sort out problems. Particular thanks go to Simon Fountain, Martin O'Shea and Harry Jack who patiently and independently read through, and commented on, the text and helped with queries, information and advice. Others who provided help and assistance or read and commented on sections of the text include Huw Edwards, Dave Pennington, Roy Thomson, Ken Wood, John Mileson, Bob Williams, Mike Williams, David Patrick, Peter Davis, Geoff Nix, Mike Wheelwright, Roger Bell, Peter Stanton and Ian Fraser. Especially important was Peter Meyer who took the large pile of material and turned it into something the printers could use. Outside the Society particular thanks are due to John Clarke of the National Railway Museum and Brian Dotson of the Stephenson Locomotive Society.

I hope that you will find the contents interesting and that they will inspire more research, writing and model-making, not to mention new volunteers to help with Society activities. Can even more be achieved in the next forty years?

Richard Foster

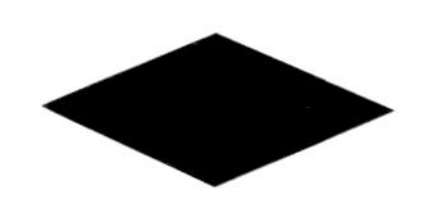

The deep sandstone cutting and bridges on the approaches to Liverpool Lime Street station on Dave Pennington's Lime Street model. This is actually a 'cut down' version of the real thing (for obvious space reasons!) with two approach tracks rather than four. The signal gantry controls access to the station platforms from the down line. Note how the gantry has been built into notches in the cutting walls, and the construction details. The right hand track with the engine is the station headshunt siding. The up line is in a tunnel to the right (as for the up slow line on the real thing) and the circular hole in front of the signal gantry provides ventilation to the tunnel, hence the smoke staining above. (Dave Pennington)

THE LNWR SOCIETY - FORTY YEARS OF PROGRESS

It is forty years since the London & North Western Railway Society was formed. This special publication celebrates the occasion and tells something of the story of what the Society and its members have achieved.

It all began back in 1973. Life-long LNWR enthusiast, Eric Rayner, frustrated over the difficulties of obtaining information about his favourite railway company, decided that a society was needed to bring together people of like interests and provide a forum for exchanging and disseminating information. He took the bold step of arranging a meeting to discuss the idea. This took place at the public library in Crewe (a very fitting geographical location for such a proposal!) on the 3rd July 1973. A small group assembled and after lively discussion agreed that a society should be formed with some very simple objectives:

'The objects of the Society are to preserve the memory of and to publicise the activities of the London & North Western Railway Company.'

This is still the basis for the Society and its activities today. The Society was officially set up on 29th September 1973 and there were around 30 members in 1974. From these small beginnings the Society has progressively grown, and today membership stands at just over 700.

Looking back, the Society has achieved an impressive amount. Four aspects of the Society's activities and achievements stand out:

- The countless friendships that have been made, often lifelong, between the various individual members;
- The Study Centre at Kenilworth and the ever growing volume of invaluable historical material and reference works housed there, a massively important resource;
- The Society's photographic collection, which now runs to many thousands of images - and is still growing;
- The output of printed material - primarily the *Journal* and its predecessors, and the publications with their valuable and informative contents.

All these are a tribute to our various officers and the people who have helped and supported them.

A very significant achievement came in 2005 when Charitable Status was granted. As part of the process a new constitution was approved by the members. Section C1 defines the 'Objects of the Society' as:

'To advance the education of the public in all aspects of the London and North Western Railway, including the study and preservation of information, drawings, photographs, models and other material pertaining to the railway company and related organisations and subjects.'

These objectives have been the focus of the Society's publications and activities, and continued in this publication. However, the Society itself is much more about people. It is people who make the Society what it is and what it has done, by volunteering and giving freely of their time and expertise. This special publication enables us to take a look at some of the people past and present who have made the Society what it is and contributed to our knowledge and understanding of the LNWR by published work and models.

While it is not a modelling group, a significant number of members are modellers, and a section takes a peek at a few of these, their models and how their modelling activities have been influenced by membership. Models are used extensively to illustrate members' achievements and describe aspects of the LNWR.

Jack Nelson and Jim Richards set out to create a visual record of the LNWR with models. Their exceptional models and their life histories are celebrated.

Finally we remember some of our former members, no longer with us, who made great contributions to our knowledge of the LNWR, or to the development of the Society (or both!).

We hope that you will find the contents of this celebratory publication an interesting and enjoyable read, and that the next forty years will be at least as productive!

The President and Vice-Presidents.

Roger Stapleton (President 2012-3)
Peter Skellon (President 2013-4)

Peter Chatham
Richard Foster
Harry Jack
Barry Lane
Andy Lowe
Martin O'Shea
Clive Taylor
Roy Thomson
Mike Williams

One of Jim Richards' more unusual models. This is a portable gas receiver or gas tank wagon. They were used to replenish the gas tanks on gas-lit carriages at remote locations that did not have their own carriage gas supply. They were also used to recharge the gas tanks on dining cars with gas-cooking equipment and gas-lit departmental vehicles. This one was 21ft 0in long on a 12ft 0in wheelbase (using the same underframe as 21ft 0in OCTs and CCTs) and could hold 444 cubic feet of gas. It was built in 1897 and assigned to Bletchley. It would probably have been used to replenish carriages stabled overnight at Oxford. It later moved to Whitehaven/Carlisle, probably after the Bletchley District sets were converted to electric light in 1906. It was classified as non-passenger coaching stock, rather than a wagon and hence was vacuum braked, the letter 'A' on the solebar indicating the position of the brake release valve. The LNWR was a leader in the conversion of carriage lighting from gas to electric, starting a conversion programme in 1914, but the work took many years. The LMS put in hand an accelerated programme for the remainder of its fleet after the Charfield accident in 1928. This wagon became LMS 05392 (the 0 indicates the supplementary list) and probably survived WW2.

(Courtesy National Railway Museum)

Jim Richards' model of an LNWR Diagram 17B 20-ton brake van. They were known as 'Crystal Palaces' on account of their larger end windows. A total of 539 of these were built over the period from 1917 to 1923 and a few lasted into BR days. The body was 18ft long by 7ft 8½in wide (8ft 5in over the guard's ogee). They were probably the only type of brake built after 1917 and all were built as replacements for scrapped vehicles. Note that on these vehicles the side lights were projected through a hole in the centre of the side, just above the ogee.

(Courtesy National Railway Museum)

EDUCATIONAL ACTIVITIES

SOCIETY PUBLICATIONS

The Society's primary means of communicating with its members is through its *Journal* and *Newsletter*. The *Journal* is published four times a year and is issued free to members. Each issue consists of about 40 pages and is A4 size, fully illustrated and printed on good quality paper. Some issues are now in colour. There are articles on a wide range of topics. Debate on the topics featured, or being researched, and the provision of further information through the readers' letters column is encouraged. The 'Press Digest' section contains details of material of interest that has appeared in external publications.

Special publications are published from time to time. These are usually on a single topic, and are well-illustrated quality productions.

Publication length varies according to subject matter, from slim productions of around 20 pages through to a 136 page hardback book. We have also reprinted several historically valuable documents in order to make them available to a wider audience. Many of our publications have been issued free to members as well as being available for purchase. There have been some 30 publications to date, forming a valuable source of information relating to the LNWR. A full list of our publications, including our flagship hardback *L&NWR Non-Corridor Carriages*, can be found in the Appendix at the end of this book. Copies of some are still available, see the Society web site for details.

THE STUDY CENTRE, LIBRARY AND ARCHIVES

By Dave Pennington

The Study Centre is named in honour of Jeremy Flegg, whose bequest to the Society provided much of the funding for setting it up.

The Library started in January 1980 with just a few books and pamphlets that could be stored in a cardboard box, and the appointment of the first Librarian. By the early 1990s the number of books had grown, mainly by donations and bequests, to the point that it was no longer feasible to carry it about.

Our library collection, grown largely from bequests, now comprises almost 900 books covering all aspects of the LNWR, its history and operation. We also have a large collection of periodical articles, either as bound volumes or as individual articles. For example we have complete sets of *Railway Magazine* from 1897 to 1973, *Railway and Travel Monthly* from 1910 to 1922, *LNWR Gazette* (the LNWR staff magazine) and *Locomotive Magazine*. The library books are all listed on our web site and there is a book bibliography on the web site that lists over 1160 books of LNWR interest. These lists are held in databases at our Study Centre.

The bibliographies of books and periodical articles began with an appeal for contributions in 1978 and a computer-based bibliography was started in 1987. Since then the bibliography has expanded greatly and now lists almost 22300 articles in a wide range of magazines and newspapers. All of the articles in the Society publications are listed. The database also shows which of these articles we have at the Study Centre, now amounting to some 16000 and still growing! The periodicals bibliography is also available on the web site, which is now the only practical means of making the information widely available.

The Archives really began in 1980 with the donation of a collection of Liverpool & Manchester documents for exhibition at the L&M 150 celebrations. The collection grew significantly during the 1990s and the Records & Relics Subcommittee was set up in 2000 to look for premises where the collections could be made available for research, and to manage the collection and the acquisition of new material.

The first places considered were the NRM at York, and various record offices. However at that time the NRM was unable to make new material available. Contact with the County Record Offices indicated that they were only really interested in material relevant to their area. This would have resulted in the collections being dispersed across the counties that the LNWR served, making use difficult and defeating the object of bringing the material together in the first place.

Between 2006 and 2008 the collection was moved to a commercial self-storage unit. While access was easy for the Librarian it was not possible for anyone else to view the material. A number of premises options were investigated, but all proved abortive. When Richard Powell offered space in his business premises in Kenilworth we decided to move the collections there and give the Study Centre idea a trial. We took on a licence to occupy two rooms, moving in on 1st December 2008. The number of visitors averaged about two to three at each monthly opening until late 2011, when numbers increased to five or six.

In early 2012 Richard Powell decided not to renew his lease on the whole premises and we decided to take on the lease from April 2012 for up to three years. This gave us much more space for the study area and more storage room. For the last couple of years we have been examining other locations for our Study Centre, among which are Nuneaton and Rugby Stations, Ironbridge Gorge Museum and a Crewe Council building.

The Study Centre reading and meeting room with Dave Pennington hard at work on the archive catalogue.

USING THE STUDY CENTRE

The Study Centre is equipped with two computers running the databases. One of them also runs the searchable Society Photographic Catalogue. There is broadband internet access and visitors with suitably equipped computers can use the free wireless internet access on the site. We have an A3 printer/scanner/copier, an A4 printer and an A4 book scanner for copying and printing material as required. Free tea and coffee making facilities are provided for visitors' use.

The collections now consist of some 4700 documents and 1900 drawings covering a huge range of subjects. These are all listed in computer databases held the Study Centre and published as PDF files on the Society web site. There are also a large number of photograph albums.

While our collections are there for research, considerable pleasure can also be gained just from browsing and visitors are welcome at the Study Centre for either purpose. Opening dates and directions can be found in the Newsletter and on the Society web site, along with details of several extra events there that we are planning.

LONDON & NORTH WESTERN AND GREAT WESTERN
JOINT RAILWAYS.
DIAGRAM OF CARRIAGE WORKING.
JULY 12 to SEPTEMBER 30, 1915, inclusive.

M—Mondays excepted. MSO—Mondays and Saturdays only. SO—Saturdays only. MO—Mondays only. FO—Fridays only. TO—Tuesdays only. MFO—Mondays and Fridays only. S—Saturdays excepted. WO—Wednesdays only.

First page of a *Diagram of Carriage Working* book for the LNWR and GWR Birkenhead & Shrewsbury Joint lines for the Summer of 1915. This details the carriage sets used on each timetabled passenger service and the daily working of each of the sets. In recent years the Society has managed to acquire a number of these very useful, but unfortunately rather rare, documents. The layout gives an indication of why they were called Diagrams (as they still are today).

(Archive Ref: MCIR024)

An LNWR permanent way maintenance diagram for Blaenau Festiniog. The archive contains several books of these maintenance diagrams and private siding diagrams. (Archive Ref: PLAN043)

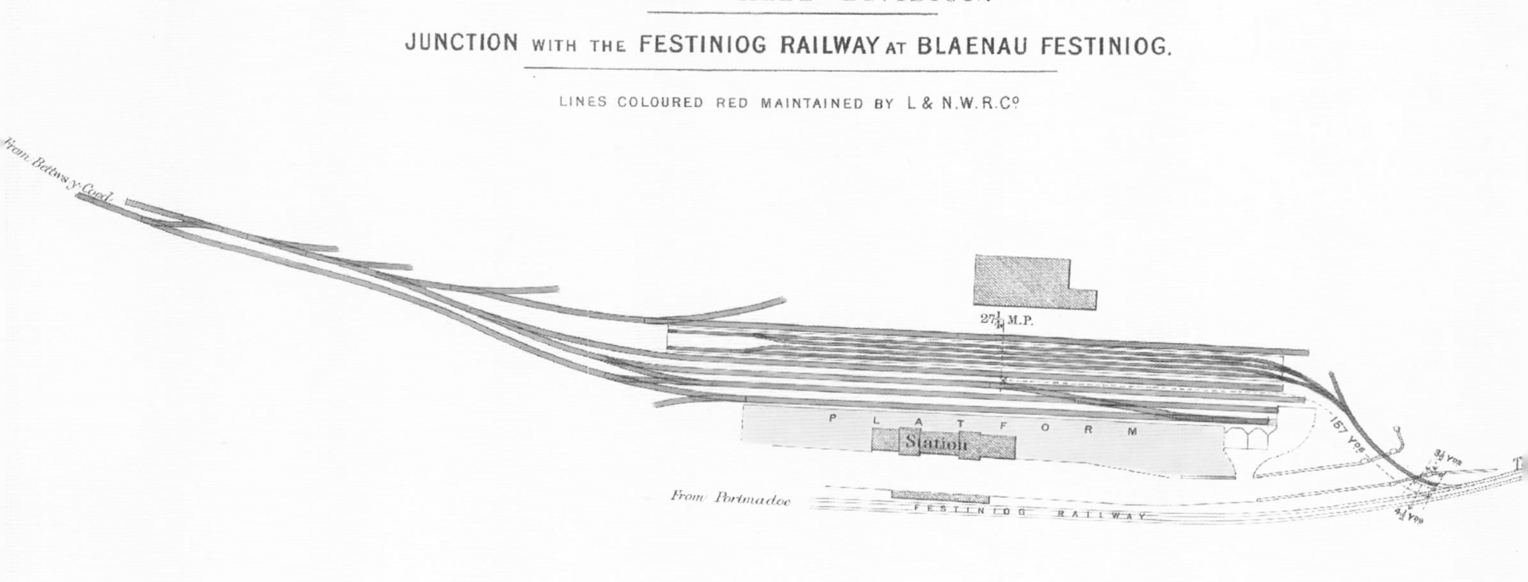

THE SOCIETY PHOTOGRAPHIC COLLECTION

By Norman Lee

Building a collection of LNWR photographs was an early objective for the Society. Mike Bland became Photographic Officer in 1975 and the initial priority was to build up a set of 35mm copy negatives using prints owned by members and friends. Much of the copying was done by F W (Tim) Shuttleworth and by the early 1980s the Society had around 2000 copy negatives. David Ratcliffe had the task of assimilating new negatives into the collection and adding material to the typed lists for members, a difficult and tedious job in pre-computer days. The lists eventually ran to several hundred pages. Printing was done to order by Tim Shuttleworth, with orders administered by Mike. I took over as Photographic Officer in 1988.

Ernie Dutton, who worked in the Drawing Office at Crewe, had acquired hundreds of old LNWR official photographs when the office closed in the 1960s and he gave these photographs to the Society. Many of them were contact prints off the original glass negatives, some of which were huge (the 'A' series were 15x12inches) so the quality was superb. Another LNWR Society member, Ray Ellis, also worked in the Drawing Office and presented another large batch of different official prints to the Society in 2000. With other donations and purchases we now have a very respectable collection of official photographs at the Study Centre.

A small part of the photograph print collection at the Study Centre.

The Society has also been fortunate with donations from private collections. These have included glass plate negatives from H A White, Dudley Whitworth's collection of over 5000 prints, over 1000 prints from David Ratcliffe and B W Leslie's negatives of LNWR sites. The Society also purchased J M Dunn's collection of negatives. Some photos have been acquired as complete collections - for example from Nevill Reid, John Shelley, Vic Forster and David Goodwin's pictures of Chester Shed, while Ted Lloyd provided scanned images from his own collection. All of these are catalogued by the originator's name.

Recent acquisitions have been John Crawley's collection - over twenty volumes of beautifully presented prints - Tim Shuttleworth's collection, and Bernard Matthews' photographs of LNWR stations and copy negatives. At various auctions the Society has bought over 2000 prints of ex-LNWR infrastructure.

When I took over as Photographic Officer the initial priority was to transfer the photograph list to a computer database. Priorities are now cataloguing new material and digitising the collection. Following advice from Peter Chatham, our current standard for scanning is to have 300 to 400 pixels per inch at the size of the printed image, so that large images can be printed. High density scans allow us to zoom in and print details of a picture. Once photographs have been scanned, the database system lets the user display a picture alongside the text description.

The John Crawley photo collection albums.

The task of scanning and cataloguing seems endless - the Society is acquiring new material faster than it can handle what it has already got. A small group of members is steadily at work. More help is always welcome. Volunteers will be given help in getting started and all the skills can easily be learnt.

Much of the Society's photograph list is available on the web site and more is being added. Images that have been digitised can be viewed. All our photographic printing is done digitally through a commercial organisation - Zenfolio - which can be reached through the Society web site. A copy of the full photograph database and a set of scanned images is kept on computer at the Study Centre and can be used by anyone who visits. Many of the original photographs and negatives are kept there too.

The Premier Line Award By Jol Wilkinson

The LNWR Society's Premier Line Award is made to an organisation or individual whose voluntary activities have contributed significantly to public awareness of the history of the LNWR. Nominations are invited from members for consideration by the committee. So far the award has been made on three occasions.

Peter Stanton presents the first of our Premier Line Awards to Andrew Dow (left), President of the Stephenson Locomotive Society, at the National Railway Museum, York, in December 2009. It was given for their work in restoring the 9 ½inch gauge Crewe Works built live steam model of Webb 4-4-0 'Alfred the Great' 4-cylinder compound 1957 *Orion*.

Introduced in 2009, the PLA was first presented to the Stephenson Locomotive Society for their outstanding contribution to LNWR history by restoring the live steam scale model locomotive *Orion*, originally built at Crewe Works by G R S Darroch. With so few LNWR locomotives having reached the 21st century, the Society felt that restoration to working order of this one-sixth scale model fully deserved our recognition. The award was made by the Society's Chairman, Peter Stanton, at the NRM.

In 2010 the Society presented the PLA to the Buckingham Railway Centre at Quainton Road, to recognise their outstanding work in the restoration of the Rewley Road Station building, the LNWR Dining and Sleeping Carriages, and other valuable historical artefacts. The presentation was made by Jol Wilkinson to Allan Baker, Chairman of the Quainton Railway Society.

The most recent award of the PLA was made to the Bahamas Locomotive Society in 2012, to commemorate their work in restoring the LNWR Webb Coal Tank 1054 to working order. At the same time the Society also presented a set of specially commissioned loco lamps, to the original LNWR design, to use on the Coal Tank on special occasions. The presentation was made by Society Chairman Peter Stanton to Mark Winderbank, Chairman of the BLS.

The Society is committed to recognizing those who have given of their time and energy to increase awareness of the LNWR. If you would like to nominate an organisation or individual whom you feel should be recognised for their efforts, please advise the Society's Promotional Officer or the Society Secretary. In particular, we would like to hear about those individuals whose work may not have been as prominent as those mentioned above, but who are deserving of recognition.

In 2012 the Society presented the PLA to the Bahamas Locomotive Society for the high quality work they had done in restoring Coal Tank 1054. For some years the Society had run an appeal to fund the manufacture of a set of replica LNWR locomotive lamps to be used with this engine. Opportunity was taken to present the PLA and the lamps to the BLS at the same time. The photograph shows the award plaque and two of the lamps (in their locomotive sockets!).

·l Wilkinson (left) presents the PLA to llan Baker, Chairman of the Quainton ailway Society, in front of the superbly ·constructed and restored Rewley Road tation in 2010. It was given for their ork in the restoration of the LNWR ·xford station and Dining and Sleeping ırriages.

·*rion* in all its glory in steam at the NRM Shildon in May 2011. It was built in the 1905 to 1912 period, with much of the ·ork undertaken at Crewe Mechanics Institute and (unofficially!) Crewe Works. The instigator, designer, part builder and ·wner was Richard Darroch, Crewe Apprentice and later Works Manager. It was not a pure 'Alfred' as Darroch modified the ·esign to incorporate a 'Precursor' type boiler, possibly because of its greater steam-raising properties. It is one-sixth scale ·nd 9 ½ inch gauge. Restoration cost around £15,000 and was made possible by a 50% grant from the Heritage Lottery Fund, ·e remainder coming from the SLS. George Richard Sutton Darroch also wrote *'Deeds of a Great Railway'* concerning the ·NWR during the Great War, and published in 1920. (Simon Fountain)

Orion and the LNWR Society
An additional note by Richard Foster

It is very fitting that the first Premier Line Award was for the restoration of *Orion* as the work had a close connection to our Society. The SLS portion of the restoration cost largely came from bequests to them from Charles Shorto and Harold Bowtell. Both were LNWR Society members. E H C Shorto was a Crewe Apprentice not long after the Grouping and later shedmaster at a number of locations. I corresponded with him over his time as an 'Improver' at Rugby, where he had taken a particular interest in the relationship between drivers and signals. Harold Bowtell was very active in the SLS and MLS in the North-West and a personal friend. He wrote a number of books and I had the pleasure of spending a lot of time helping him with, and reviewing the text for, his *Over Shap to Carlisle* and *Rails Through Lakeland Fells*. They were two of life's gentlemen of fond memory, and without them the restoration of *Orion* might not have been possible.

Orion, resplendent in the sunshine while visiting the Downs Light Railway in April 2005, shortly after the restoration work had been completed. The SLS certainly did a magnificent job on it. The loco is now at Locomotion, the National Railway Museum at Shildon, and is steamed from time to time for special events. (N R Knight, courtesy SLS)

The rocker levers under *Orion's* front cover. The arrangements on the 4-cylinder 4-4-0s and "Claughtons" were similar.

(Simon Fountain)

(Copyright: N R Knight)

Steam-Ups By Ken Wood

LNWR liveries, steam and movement, the Steam-Ups are a lovely opportunity to relive the LNWR! Mike Wheelwright is driving his 5inch gauge model of 'Claughton' 650 *Lord Rathmore* at the 2009 Steam-Up. Fittingly for this Anniversary publication the LNWR locomotive was completed 100 years ago in June 1913. This was Mike's 5th model and took 8 years to build, being completed in 2008. The scale is 1 1/16inches to a foot and it has four cast iron cylinders 1 3/8 x 2 ¼inches with ¾inch diameter piston valves, all with multiple rings. The Belpaire boiler has a working pressure of 90psi. It can pull a 1000 lb train at 3 mph up a 1 in 75 gradient at 50% cut off. Mike says this is equivalent to passing Scout Green with 600 tons at 35 mph. Pretty good stuff! He is now well on with his next loco 1045 *Whitworth.* (Richard Foster)

We have a number of members who are practising model engineers. Once a year we have a *Steam-Up* where they can run their locomotives and where members can come along to see the machines in action and join in the fun. Planning for each event takes about a year.

The inaugural event took place in September 2001 and was hosted by the Erewash Valley Model Engineering Society of which my friend Nigel Thompson is a founder member. This event has grown over the years and we always try to find a society in the Midlands who is prepared to host it as the central location means that as many people as possible can get there. We have had people coming from such diverse places as Worthing, Exeter, Grimsby, Blackpool, Leyland, Bradford, Huddersfield, Suffolk and Norfolk.

After Erewash in 2001, we were invited to Sutton Coldfield Model Engineering Society in 2002 and this was so successful that we went again in 2003. In 2004 we were at the Leicester Society, in 2005 at my own Stafford and District Model Engineering Society and in 2006 the Birmingham Society of Model and Experimental Engineers did the honours. In 2007 it was the turn of the South Cheshire Model Engineering Society. We returned to Sutton Coldfield in 2008 and Birmingham in 2009, followed by Erewash in 2010 and Kinver and West Midlands MES in 2011. 2012 saw us return to South Cheshire. All of these clubs have excellent facilities and make us really welcome.

Over the years we have been blessed with truly wonderful weather, with one exception, Stafford in 2005, but we model engineers are a hardy lot and just got on with it. At Leicester in 2004 it started to rain about 5pm. Roger Bell managed to get the track to himself and was speeding around when the heavens opened and dumped a very heavy shower upon him, but he just carried on driving his lovely 3 ½inch gauge engine!

Dave Roberts hard at work with his 5inch gauge model of Webb 'Teutonic' three-cylinder compound 1304 *Jeanie Deans* at the 2007 Steam-Up. Dave has been a regular participant at the Steam-Ups.

(Simon Fountain)

Roger Bell in characteristic pose doing a final check round 'Teutonic' 1311 *Celtic* at the September 2002 Sutton Coldfield Steam-Up while Brenda Lawson operates Roger's 'patent' portable water tower. This 3½inch gauge model was built by John Hill and finished by Roger, but is now back with John. The boiler was built by Alec Farmer of Solihull and is pressed to 120psi, which allows for the drop in pressure between the high and low pressure cylinders and makes the loco's performance quite lively. Roger says it roars wonderfully when in full flight! 'Teutonic' 2-2-2-0 compound *Celtic* was built in June 1890 and scrapped in March 1906. (Tony Gillam)

Bill Finch's splendid 5inch gauge model of 'Renewed Precedent' or 'Jumbo' 1194 *Miranda*. The LNWR loco was built in 1897 and became LMS 5068 in 1928. (LNWRS MDL002)

The Crewe Luncheon

By Ken Wood

Towards the end of the 1980s some members suggested that there should be an informal gathering with no formal Society business. From discussions the idea emerged to hold a luncheon with a speaker giving a talk in the afternoon and I was asked if I would organise it. A venue was needed and the Crewe Arms seemed ideal, with its strong LNWR associations. The management at the Crewe Arms were very receptive to the idea and gave advice and encouragement. I chose a suitable menu and the event was advertised in the Newsletter. Next, I needed a speaker. Gordon Webster had put together a light hearted look at the LNWR and agreed to give a presentation.

That the luncheon was successful can be judged by this comment from the late Eric Russell: 'The postprandial talk was hugely enjoyable. Apart from the unusual and interesting pictures, which gave rise to so much useful comment, it was refreshingly light hearted. In short it was a salutary lesson to us all not to take our obsession too seriously.' Thirty-eight people sat down to a three-course luncheon that day in November 1990 and suitably encouraged I set about planning the second for November 1991.

London & North Western Railway Society

Sir Richard Moon (1815-1899)
vincit omnia veritas

Richard Foster

The Crewe Luncheon
Saturday, November 18th 2000

Over the years the luncheons, which are held on the third Saturday in November, have grown considerably with attendances now in the sixties. I have managed to maintain a very high standard with help from the management of the Crewe Arms and their dedicated staff. This year will be the 24th luncheon held there and it is my hope that it will continue to be a popular event in the calendar, and I am happy to carry on organising them.

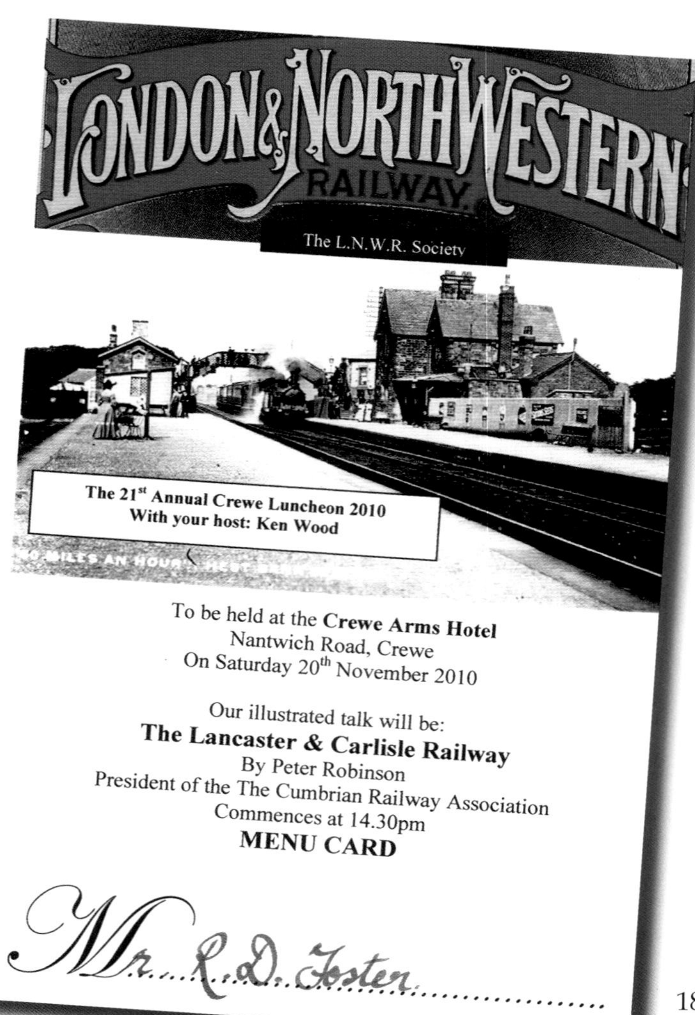

CREWE LUNCHEONS – SPEAKERS AND TOPICS

YEAR	SPEAKER	TOPIC
1990	Gordon Webster	A light-hearted look at the LNWR
1991	Allan Baker	My days at Crewe Sheds
1992	Charles Taylor	Life at a Loco Works: Crewe
1993	Peter Davis	Webb Compounds
1994	Harold Bowtell	The LNWR around Lancaster
1995	Niall Ferguson	The Dundee and Newtyle Railway
1996	Don Rowland	A retrospective look at the LNWR in Crewe
1997	Peter Lee	Nuneaton and the Trent Valley Railway
1998	Allan Rimmer	The Cromford & High Peak Railway Part 1
1999	Allan Rimmer	The Cromford & High Peak Railway Part 2
2000	Peter Braine	Sir Richard Moon
2001	Malcolm Reed	The LNWR in Retrospect (based around his 1996 book)
2002	Robin Pennie	John Ramsbottom
2003	Philip Atkins	Number Crunching: An analytical view of loco building at Crewe
2004	Bob Yate	The Shropshire Union Railway
2005	Norman Lee	Magic Lantern slides
2006	Graham Hardy	The Leeds Road Part 1
2007	Steve Weston	The Rugby upgrade and rebuilding of the station
2008	Graham Hardy	The Leeds Road Part 2
2009	Robin Callup & Jim Chesney	The GNR & LNWR Joint Line Market Harborough to Colwick
2010	Peter Robinson	The Lancaster and Carlisle Railway
2011	Dr Michael Bailey	Joseph Locke: The Third Engineer
2012	Geoffrey Bott	The Cockermouth Keswick & Penrith Railway

643

MODELLING THE LNWR

A lovely shot of Denis Nix's Webb 'Dreadnought' compound 2-2-2-0 showing the cab backhead and toolbox detail. Note the stanchion for the passenger alarm cord on the far side of the tender. LNWR 643 *Raven* was built in 1888 and scrapped in October 1904. The model represents it in its later condition.
(Courtesy Geoff Nix)

MODELLING THE LNWR

The primary object of the Society is the study and preservation of information about the LNWR and its dissemination. While the study and preservation of models is acknowledged as a means of education, the introductory text in some of the Society's publications states 'Although not a modelling Society, the membership includes the builders of some well-known layouts and models'.

This publication gives an opportunity to look at some of our modeller members and what they do. Each was asked to write a short piece on why they model the LNWR, the way in which membership of the Society has helped them, and a little bit about themselves. We start with some notes by our 2012-2013 President, Roger Stapleton. Interestingly both Roger and Simon Fountain have chosen to portray steam sheds. Simon's notes therefore follow Roger's as different approaches to the same theme, but the other contributions are in no particular order. The models are inspiring!

MODELLING THE LNWR - MY PERSONAL JOURNEY

By Roger Stapleton

You have to be a determined sort of person to model the LNWR in any scale because little is available for buying 'off the shelf'. Therefore you have to build it yourself, either from scratch or with the aid of kits. Fortunately, there is a huge range of kits available for you to choose from and the 'Modelling' area of the Society web site attempts to list them all! A modeller also needs accurate and accessible information and this is readily available in the form of books and from the Society's publications and archives.

Given these difficulties, why would anyone choose to model the LNWR? For myself, this is 'because of its superb looks'. I first became aware of the LNWR when I was seventeen and I saw the illustrations in 'Premier Line' by O.S.Nock. I was fascinated by the weird shiny black engines and resolved there and then that, one day, I would build models of them. Unfortunately, then you had to build such models from scratch and, not having the skill, I put the idea to one side. Forty years later it resurfaced and, to my delight, I discovered that a host of kits were available which were within my competence - and I have been building them ever since!

A 'Lady of the Lake' class 2-2-2 1430 *Pandora*, on the up main line, is hauling a private train hired by a member of the aristocracy to convey his family, servants, horses, carriage and accoutrements to Scotland for the season. Coal Engine 713 is proceeding onto the turntable, whilst in the background a permanent-way train, headed by a 4ft 6in 2-4-2 Tank, is departing after having deposited a consignment of new rails. *Pandora* was built from a K's kit of 1970s vintage. The Coal Engine is from a kit by London Road Models and the 4ft 6in 2-4-2T is from a Perseverance kit. The twin-bore tunnel is based on the one at Vaynol, between Bangor and Caernarvon. The main lines model the obsolete 30ft lengths of rail. The ballast covers the sleepers in the old-fashioned way. The signal on the down line has a fixed distant. (Photo Steve Flint courtesy of Railway Modeller)

busy day at the Steam Shed! 'Dreadnought' class 2-2-2-0 three-cylinder compound 2059 *Greyhound* and 'Bill Bailey' class -0 four-cylinder compound No 1113 await their turns at the coal stage. A 4ft 6in 2-4-2 Tank, having been coaled and watered, ads off for work, whilst a 'Lady of the Lake' 2-2-2 and a 'Cauliflower' 0-6-0 await their turns of duty. The 'Dreadnought' is ilt from an M&L kit. The 'Bill Bailey' is from a much modified London Road Models kit for the 'C/C1' class 0-8-0. The 2-4-2T rom a Perseverance kit, and the 'Cauliflower' is from a kit by GEM. (Photo Steve Flint courtesy of Railway Modeller)

'A' class three-cylinder compound 0-8-0 1867 passes the steam shed on the down line with a train of private-owner coal gons, whilst 'Special Tank' 0-6-0ST 3368 makes its way to the coal stage. Outside the shed office a 'Bowler Hat' (Shed reman!) surveys the scene. On the far side of the tracks steam ploughing is taking place. 1867 was built in 1899 and rebuilt class C1 in 1909, while 3368 was a duplicate list number. The 0-8-0 was built from a much modified London Road Models for the 'A' class 0-8-0, and the 'Special Tank' is from a kit by the same maker. Two kits from Premier Kits were combined construct the steam shed. The surplus pieces from these kits were utilised for the long factory building in the background d for the blacksmiths' workshop. (Photo Steve Flint courtesy of Railway Modeller)

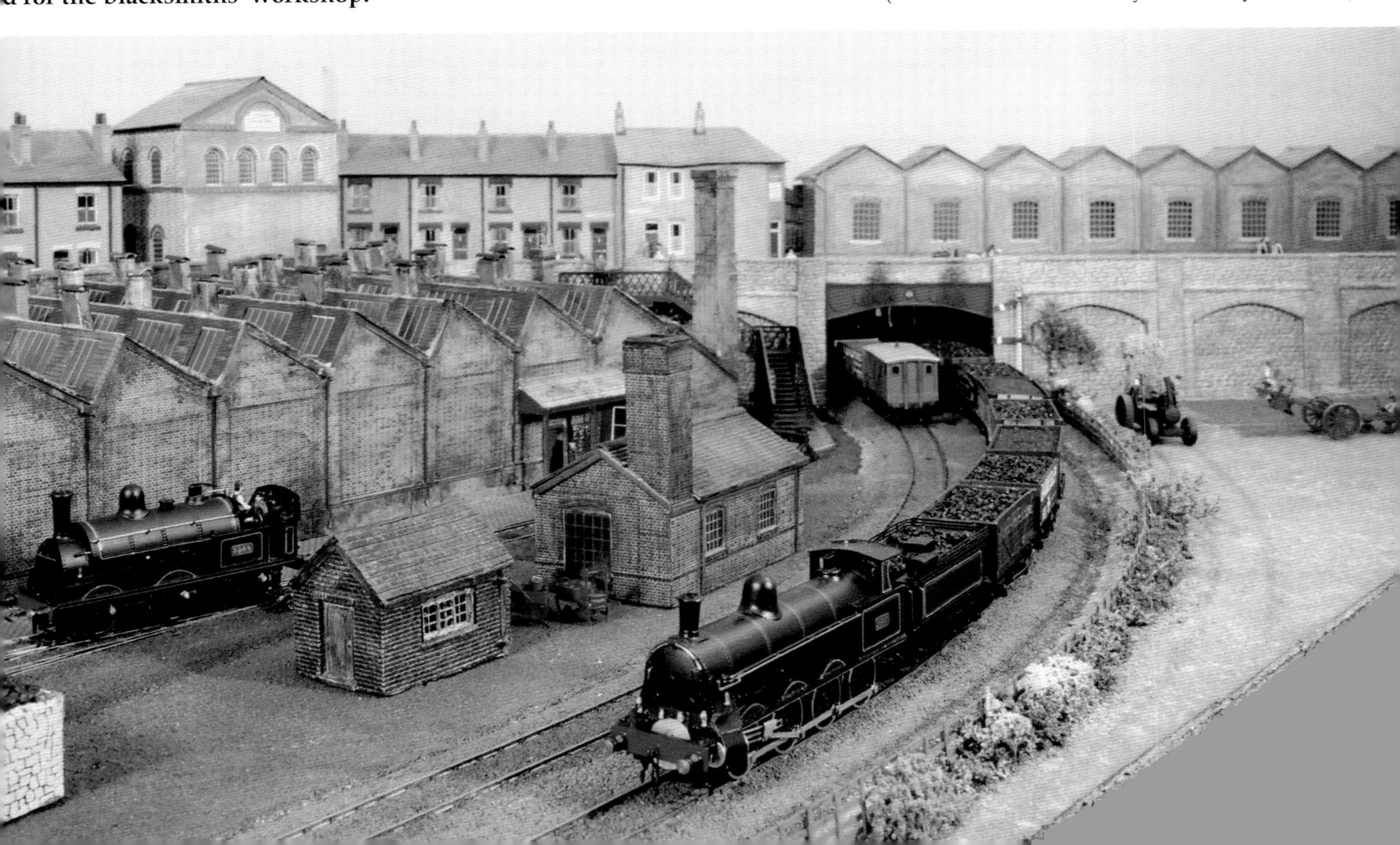

'Jubilee' class four-cylinder compound 4-4-0 1903 *Iron Duke* has been coaled and watered and is ready for a hard day's work. The LNWR loco was the first of the 'Jubilee' compounds, completed in March 1899, and was rebuilt as a 'Renown' in May 1924. The loco was built from the London Road Models kit. The coal stage was scratch-built using information from the book *LNWR Portrayed* by Jack Nelson. (Photo Steve Flint courtesy of Railway Modeller)

Having built some models, what do you then do with them? You can have them on display, but they are models of creations that moved, and transported people and goods from place to place. So I had to build a layout on which to run my models and, having built it, what could I do with it? My response was to take it to model railway exhibitions all over the country to give the spectators some idea of what the LNWR might have looked like over 100 years ago. It is only a brief and passing glimpse but it is probably as near as we will ever get to an era when railways were the supreme mode of transport and the LNWR considered itself to be the Premier Line.

My layout is constructed to a scale of 4mm/ft. It has a frontage of 12 feet and a depth of 8 feet. It comprises an engine shed ('steam shed' in LNWR parlance) with a double-track main line passing in front of it. Eight trains of various types run along the main line while many locomotives of other classes enter, leave or potter around the shed. There is, therefore, always something in motion to interest the viewer. It has been on display at 24 exhibitions during the past ten years and has now, probably, been retired - not because it has reached its sell-by date but because the team of operators have! Exhibiting a model railway is hard work but it is also a rewarding experience. The viewing public are very appreciative of what they see and are often more knowledgeable than the operators. We have handed out numerous LNWRS application forms and hopefully some have been inspired to join the Society.

Roger's layout has its own website www.lnwrsteamshed.co.uk

If you have a look you might find something of interest.

MODELLING THE LNWR

By Simon Fountain

My reasons for joining the Society were an interest in the LNWR, particularly its distinctive locomotives, and in wanting to model these (initially in 4mm/ft scale). Over the last 26 years, my interest in all things LNWR has developed, and the modelling has progressed, although with a change up to 7mm/ft scale.

The Society publications, particularly the *Journal*, have certainly broadened my interest. This caused the construction of locos to be delayed while the buildings and infrastructure were researched and made for my 'steam shed' layout (see *Model Railway Journal* No 198). Since then, several locos have been completed, but are modelled as running in the LMS period. This was to allow Stanier locos to appear, but in reality I'll do well to complete all the LNWR locos I want to build! The *Bill Finch Portfolio* is extremely useful in getting the detail on the locos right.

Other publications produced by our members, such as Ted Talbot's *LNWR Engines*, Jack Nelson's *LNWR Portrayed* and Richard Foster's *A Pictorial Record of LNWR Signalling*' have been invaluable, plus all those publications which include photos of the LNWR scene.

I have taken the Society's sales stand to the model railway exhibitions at Wigan and Telford. At these, I have enjoyed meeting other members, talking to traders about their products relating to the LNWR, and to those manning other line society stands. Dealing with queries from the public has sometimes been challenging, but with so many knowledgeable members, it's usually easy to suggest someone who can answer more competently!

Simon Fountain's model of LNWR 'Prince of Wales' Class 4-6-0 LMS 25673 *Lusitania* standing outside his steam shed. The LNWR locomotive was built in March 1916 as LNWR 1100. It became LMS 5673 in November 1927, and 25673 in August 1934 and was scrapped in 1949. (Simon Fountain)

2-4-2 Tank LMS 6659 sits in the twilight outside an otherwise deserted shed on Simon Fountain's layout. An evocative shot, taking one back to that unmistakable steam shed smell (aroma does not seem quite the right word!) coming from the combined effect of years of gas, smoke, steam and oil! (Simon Fountain)

MODELLING THE LNWR - GETTING BETTER ALL THE TIME!

By Jol Wilkinson

Modelling the LNWR has become increasingly easy in recent years even though the Premier Line ceased to exist as a separate entity ninety years ago. We have an extensive range of high quality kits for locomotives, carriages, wagons, infrastructure, etc, especially in 4mm and 7mm scales.

Whether modelling a specific or imaginary location, capturing the look and atmosphere of the LNWR needs access to information. In addition to publications from major publishers the LNWR Society's archives, records, photographs, plans and own publications are a great asset. The Society's own on-line forum is also a useful source of information.

The Society's own publications, including *LNWR Non-Corridor Carriages* and *LNWR Wagons - Supplement No. 1*, fill in many valuable gaps not covered by the commercial sector, while Portfolios such as the *Bill Finch Portfolio of Locomotive Details*, *LNWR Company Houses* and *Thirty Foot One Inch Carriages* contain valuable details for the modeller in all scales. The Society's *Journal* is a source of inspiration and information and the Society's web site includes a modelling section with details of where information can be found, sources of photographs and what kits are available.

While extending the 4mm layout *London Road* I have been able to find information on a number of topics I couldn't find elsewhere - track details for example, as well as getting guidance on signalling. Getting the small details right is important in capturing the overall scene, so photographs showing the 'mundane' such as station furniture, signs, etc are especially useful.

The 'new' extended *London Road* should be appearing at a small number of model railway exhibitions in the next few years. If you want to know more about modelling the LNWR, especially in 4mm, please speak to any of the operating team

The locomotive spur on the *London Road* layout with 2-4-2 5ft 6in Tank 2219 with a loco coal wagon against the wooden stop blocks. Note the track and wooden staircase down to the siding from the yard above. The LNWR loco was built in 1893, became LMS 6688 in 1927, was motor fitted in 1931 and scrapped in 1951. The model of 2219 was built about 20 years ago using an M&L white metal kit and scratch built chassis to 18.83mm gauge effectively as an 0-6-2 with compensated suspension on the first two axles and a rear pony truck. Today kits are available from GEM and London Road. The loco coal wagon is a modified Ratio kit.

(Jol Wilkinson)

Webb 2-4-2 4ft 6in tank 769 in the platform at *London Road*. The LNWR loco was built in 1883 and withdrawn in October 1927. The model came from a GEM kit and is coupled to a MicroRail 30ft 1in six-wheel D359 brake third and a Mallard Models WCJS six-wheel fish van. The Mallard kit is no longer available, but a new kit for the D359 is now available from London Road Models. In the background are a D385 six-wheel brake van and two 42ft arc-roof carriages, also from London Road Models kits. In the adjacent platform line is a North London carriage set. (Jol Wilkinson)

The *London Road* station throat with the coaling stage, water column and ash pit. Note the point rodding and the timbering to provide walkways and protection to point equipment. (Jol Wilkinson)

MODELLING THE LNWR AND LIME STREET By Dave Pennington

My railway interest originates from modelling, which started with a Horny Dublo train set and developed more seriously in the late 1960s with the LMS. It regressed to the LNWR period in 1974 when I started a second, more accurate, version of my Stanmore layout. The change of period was the result of exhibiting the model and acquiring photographs of the station showing the 2-4-0T and two-coach motor set in LNWR livery and hanging flower baskets along the canopy. These photos and an LMS plan showed the early model to be quite inaccurate. The new model went on the exhibition circuit from 1974 to 1989 attending around fifty exhibitions in all. At one of the earlier exhibitions I met David Clarke who persuaded me to join the Society. Being Librarian & Archivist has expanded my interests in the LNWR beyond just modelling through the opportunity to examine our documents, drawings and photographs while cataloguing them.

In 1990, *Stanmore* was retired and another modelling project was required - one that would satisfy my desire for longer trains. After half a dozen potential stations had been examined, seeing *London Road* at an exhibition showed that a reasonable size terminus could be fitted in the space I had available. Originating from Liverpool, I had always been interested in Lime Street with its impressive vertical sandstone cuttings and after some sketching of ideas it was apparent that a much cut down 'impression' of Liverpool Lime Street in 4mm scale EM gauge was feasible.

The period of the layout was chosen to be 1900-06 as Webb locomotives would predominate but allow the use of low elliptical roof carriages, which I think are most graceful. An additional attraction was that rolling stock from various 'foreign' lines ran into Lime Street providing a colourful variety.

There then followed quite a bit of research to find out more about the track plan, the station and train sets to assist with the modelling. A spin off from this has been research into the history of the station and hotel, which has escalated from a potential article through a portfolio and into a book on the subject. Direct access to our archives has proved to be very helpful in pursuing these interests and much generous assistance with questions and information has been provided by various members.

Besides completing Lime Street, I have a number of other research projects that have captured my interest, although no doubt it will be impossible to finish them all!

A view through the bridges and tunnels to Edge Hill No 1 signal box. Although a reduced layout (two tracks instead of four) it captures very well the confined location and how the signal engineer has worked hard to get the best out of a very difficult location. The signal arms are located near the centre of the bridge arch to get the best possible view for approaching drivers, and while the signal cabin has to be overhead, it is placed as low as possible to give the signalman a bit of a view under the bridge, but not of course into the tunnels towards Edge Hill. (D Pennington)

Edge Hill No 1 signal box looking down the tunnels and bridges towards Lime Street, with the separate tunnel for the up line. Dave has modelled the original signals from 1885, while Jack Nelson (front cover) has modelled the later replacements (can you spot the difference?). (D Pennington)

The Lime Street throat looking from the platform ends showing the signal box and bridges. Note how the ground surface has been made level with the rail heads, with boarding in the four-foots. This gave a level walking surface for shunters and train crew who had to walk about the area frequently as part of normal operations and was intended to reduce tripping risk. It was asked for by the Board of Trade to help with staff safety, but the disadvantage was that track defects could not be seen and it made maintenance difficult. It was eventually removed. (D Pennington)

RESEARCHING, WRITING ABOUT AND MODELLING THE LNWR

By Philip Millard

I have been interested in the LNWR for over 60 years. I joined the Manchester Model Railway Society in 1953, and soon was privileged to get to know the late Geoff Platt. Geoff was a true authority on the LNWR, and of course knew the Pre-Grouping scene well. Geoff was enormously knowledgeable, but he tended to keep it stored in his head, where of course it was not accessible to others. That was why I made it my policy to write down the results of my researches, and publish the information wherever possible. I realised that unless I did this, no-one else would. *(This is a very pertinent point; see the comments by Kathleen Platt Page 82).*

Other people who had a profound influence on me were Jim Richards (an outstanding model maker and observer), and Geoff Williams who exhibited his *Aylesbury* EM gauge model railway layout at the 1956 MRC Exhibition. It made me realise that it was possible to construct a realistic and authentic model of an LNWR location, and gave me enormous encouragement. Jack Nelson was also a great inspiration, and I was proud to be able to contribute to his book '*LNWR Portrayed*'. Jack was another fine modeller and draughtsman.

My speciality is LNWR and WCJS passenger carriages and non-passenger coaching stock. In the 1970s I spent a lot of time at the Public Records Office at Kew, abstracting information from the Minute Books. I was also lucky enough to be allowed access to the former LNWR Wolverton Carriage Works, where I made copies of many of the drawings and LNWR records - not all of which seem to have survived. At that time the Works was still functioning and the Chief Draughsman was the late Cyril Webb, who was a mine of information and anecdotes about LNWR carriages. He ensured that these important archives were saved. The Wolverton original drawings and records entered the NRM collection around 1982, but were then inaccessible for almost 30 years, only being catalogued and made available recently.

I have been a member of the LNWRS pretty well from the outset. I am happy to have contributed many articles to the *Journal*, and have also been responsible for several publications by the Society and HMRS, not least the *Register of West Coast Joint Stock* and co-authorship of *LNWR Liveries*. I contribute to the Society's administration as the Examiner of the annual accounts. I also participate enthusiastically in the Society's on-line forum, and answer postal enquires from members seeking information about carriages.

My main focus is modelling and the research which is a necessary prelude to that. I model the LNWR in 4mm scale, EM gauge. My layout *Westborough* is a fictitious location of an important town in Lancashire, not too far from Wigan. Although fictitious I have tried to model real buildings, bridges and so on. Of course, I insist on authentic locomotives and rolling stock as well. I run two periods - 1910 (LNWR) and 1930 (LMS period), which allows me the largest possible range of locomotives and rolling stock. A model railway must balance quantity, quality, time and cost. My policy is to build my models to be as realistic and accurate as is reasonably possible, but at the same time they must have the robustness needed to survive normal usage on a working layout. In practice that means ignoring underframe detail which is not visible at three feet.

Earlier model coaches were made from Plastikard, and I still have a few of these in service. In the early 1970s I produced a range of LNWR/WCJS single-sided coach sides/ends made from processed engraved (etched) zinc. These were a huge leap forward compared with other coach 'kits' at the time, and over the years I have made about 100 carriages from these parts, some of them unusual ones such as Post Offices. Of course, these sides/ends pre-dated the more modern etched brass kits, and still needed the windows cutting out. But the extra thickness of zinc means that the windows are recessed to a more realistic depth, and zinc takes paint much better than brass. I also co-operated with Ratio, London Road Models, Chowbent and Stevenson Carriages by providing official drawings and prototype information to enable them to manufacture authentic kits.

To build models requires a reasonably well equipped workshop. I regard a vertical drilling machine as absolutely essential, and a lathe as highly desirable. Mine is a Unimat 1, bought in 1971 with the proceeds of an accountancy exam prize. Over the years I have made quite a few bespoke tools and jigs which help to speed up production. An airbrush and a good quality ruling pen are also necessary to achieve a quality paint finish. Paint undoubtedly covereth a multitude of sins!

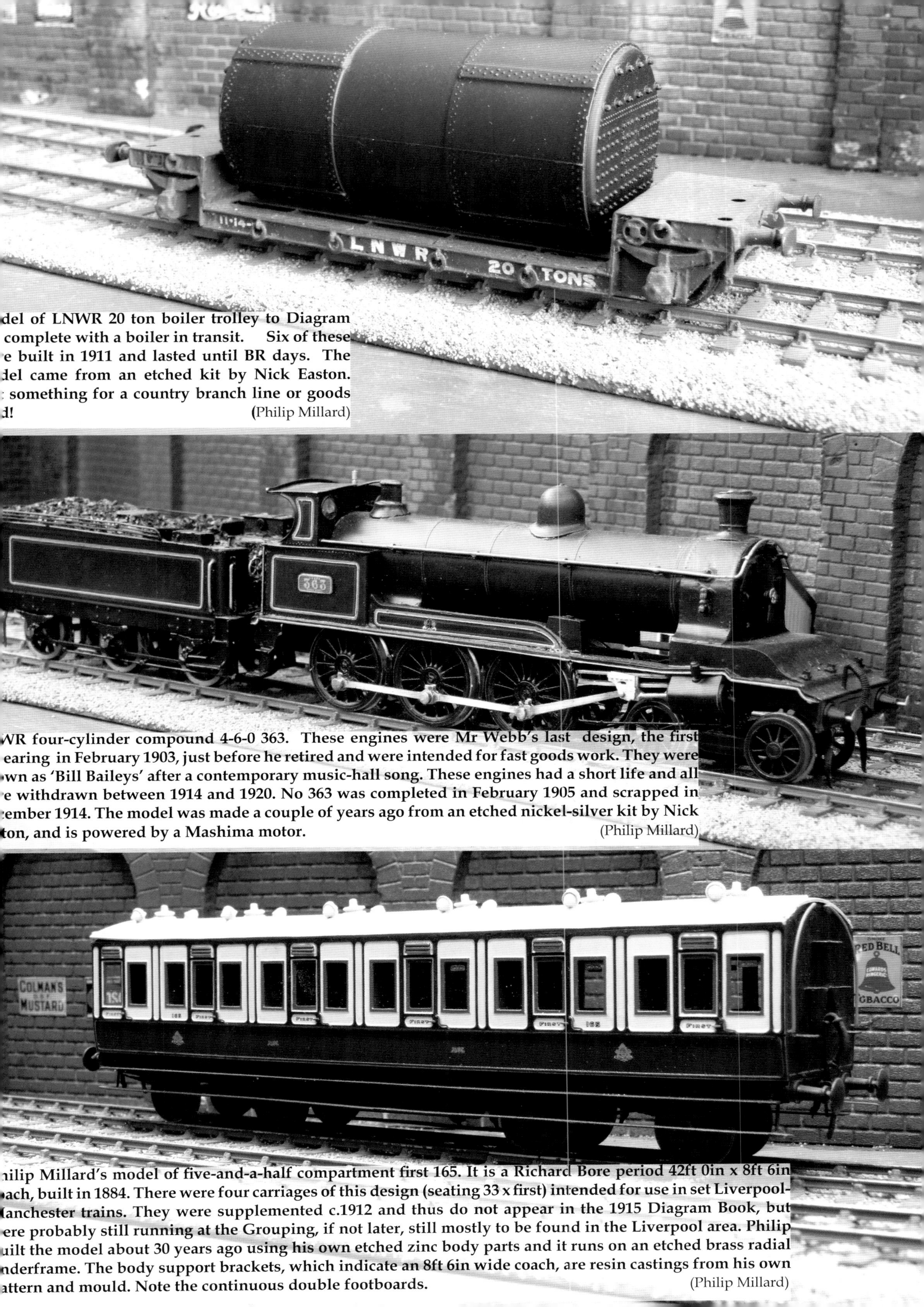

del of LNWR 20 ton boiler trolley to Diagram complete with a boiler in transit. Six of these e built in 1911 and lasted until BR days. The del came from an etched kit by Nick Easton. something for a country branch line or goods d! (Philip Millard)

WR four-cylinder compound 4-6-0 363. These engines were Mr Webb's last design, the first earing in February 1903, just before he retired and were intended for fast goods work. They were wn as 'Bill Baileys' after a contemporary music-hall song. These engines had a short life and all e withdrawn between 1914 and 1920. No 363 was completed in February 1905 and scrapped in ember 1914. The model was made a couple of years ago from an etched nickel-silver kit by Nick ton, and is powered by a Mashima motor. (Philip Millard)

hilip Millard's model of five-and-a-half compartment first 165. It is a Richard Bore period 42ft 0in x 8ft 6in ach, built in 1884. There were four carriages of this design (seating 33 x first) intended for use in set Liverpool- anchester trains. They were supplemented c.1912 and thus do not appear in the 1915 Diagram Book, but ere probably still running at the Grouping, if not later, still mostly to be found in the Liverpool area. Philip uilt the model about 30 years ago using his own etched zinc body parts and it runs on an etched brass radial nderframe. The body support brackets, which indicate an 8ft 6in wide coach, are resin castings from his own attern and mould. Note the continuous double footboards. (Philip Millard)

THE JOY OF RESEARCH AND MODELLING By John Stockton-Wood

Some thirty years ago, after visiting the Manchester Model Railway Exhibition, I considered making a start on a model railway of my own. With the problems of working in Hotels at the time, and moving about, I had no permanent home, and therefore felt the best approach was to build up a collection of quality models, when I could afford them, from respected professional modellers.

As my wish was for a branch line set in North Wales, I started researching the whole of North Wales, and after a long time settled on Llanberis for the final choice. Because my choice was of *'a real area'* I knew that accuracy demanded a lot of research. To this end, I joined the HMRS and LNWRS. After some 10 years, I felt time was right to concentrate on the models for the period I wished to model, 1900-15, as being the height of the steam age, but also offering me enough choice for the models I wished to collect.

During my early research of Llanberis I was fortunate to meet Bill Rear who was not only a fireman, based in Bangor, and worked over the line, but had also written books on North Wales branch lines. In 2005-06 I wrote two articles for our *Journal* concerning the branch line, these being based on my research so far.

During the early part of 2006, Mike Williams, the then editor of our *Journal,* had decided to retire, and I offered my services as editor; the rest is history, as I became responsible for the next twelve issues of the *Journal* – Volume 5. While acting as the editor for our *Journal,* and in discussion with both Philip Millard and Peter Chatham, it was felt a revised Portfolio of Philip's book on 30ft 1in carriages with new information would be valuable. The carriage books greatly helped me in ensuring my 7mm models were correct.

I had also managed to purchase a fine model of LNWR 17in Special DX Engine 3121, built by John Petcher. My problem was in ensuring I had correctly identified it, as Baxters' two books, *British Locomotive Catalogue 1825-1923*, Volumes 2A and 2B, had conflicting information. I therefore contacted Ted Talbot and Harry Jack, who gave me the correct information about the model.

The current trend in model railways is for DCC control along with sound, and there is no doubt both of these developments have advantages. To convert all my locomotives to DCC was not feasible for me, as it involved finding a person who could not only carry out the work, but also not damage the excellent paint work on the locomotives done by Alan Brackenborough. However, I did feel the `sound effects` were well worth pursuing and once again another Society member came to my assistance, being Simon Fountain, who suggested I contact Robert Smith who had come up with an excellent system that produced the `sound effects` that Simon was happy with for his layout.

Robert agreed to build a system for *Llanberis* and to install it, ensuring it met both his high standards and my expectations. Sounds are different for each locomotive, and Robert commented *'each locomotive starts to move at a different 'start' voltage and requires a different 'rate' of chuffs and 'cut-off' (length of chuff)'.* He therefore introduced a selector covering 12 different types of locomotive and features to cover coasting, accelerating, decelerating and train weight. Robert has also provided background sounds. For *Llanberis* these included bird songs, church bells, cow and sheep sounds, along with a guard's whistle, signal-box bells and levers being moved.

Finally I cannot finish this short article without mentioning another helpful member in the Society. This was Richard Foster, who very kindly supplied me with signalling information for *Llanberis,* along with information on how it all worked. I had no knowledge of this serious and important part of railway operations, so my model would have never been finished correctly, without his advice. Without the help of many members within the Society, over the years, I would not have been able to complete my model of Llanberis to meet with my original aspirations, so I cannot thank all of them enough.

Signalling layout for Llanberis through from LNWR to BR days.

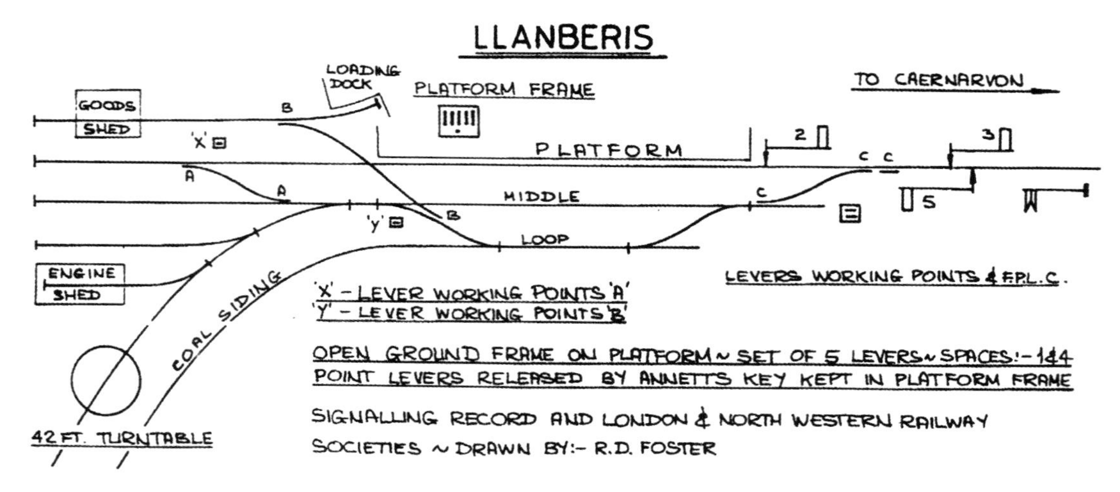

Webb 17inch Coal engine 713 in the loop at Llanberis. The original locomotive was built in March 1879, renumbered to 3330 in December 1916 and withdrawn in 1926. This is a photograph worth studying: the detail is superb. The model was built by John Petcher and features working inside valve gear. The track is modelled with 30ft rails with the later standard of 12 sleepers per length, and correctly modelled with 9ft x 10in x 5in intermediate sleepers and 12in x 5in sleepers each side of the rail joints. The track was built by Norman Soloman. (Barry Norman)

Llanberis station with Cauliflower 666 waiting to depart with a 5-carriage return excursion set. The carriages are a D360 two-compartment brake third, two 32ft luggage composites, a D197 30ft 1in luggage composite and lastly another D360 brake. The narrow wooden platform on the right is the ticket collector's platform for arriving trains. These were a feature of a number of stations in LNWR days. Note the rotating-type ground signal and hand point lever, and attention to detail is evident from the oval LNWR bridge number plate on the pier of the footbridge. The Cauliflower model was made by Peter Everton and the carriages by John Petcher. (Barry Norman)

The regular service train standing in the platform at Llanberis. The train engine is 5ft 6in tank 2184. The two carriages form part of the permanently coupled 'Llanberis set' of carriages normally used on the branch trains. The nearer vehicle is Diagram 297 all-third No 599; note the two 'Smoking' compartments, the 'Llanberis' carriage board, the quality of the painting and lining and the underframe detail. The other vehicle is a two-compartment brake third to Diagram 360. The models were built by John Petcher. (Barry Norman)

MODELLING & THE LNWR SOCIETY By Mike Williams

I grew up with a father who was ahead of his time in making a superb 4mm model of a real station in its entirety - Aylesbury LNWR. It was natural then that I emulated my father and brother Bob - himself a most accomplished modeller - but I felt I could not compete with them, so after looking briefly at N Gauge, I settled on 7mm. I joined the Gauge 0 Guild in 1969 at the age of 12 and started scratchbuilding the LNWR, mainly because the drawings and photographs were to hand, but I also used kits when the scale became popular in the 1980s and 1990s.

Through my father I was fortunate to have met many great names of the past who encouraged me, including Richards, Platt, Miller, Nix, Maskelyne, Ratcliff, Cashmore and others equally renowned but mercifully still with us, like Talbot, Millard, Jack, Lane, Chatham and Davis. Most of these were or are members of the LNWRS and many have become good friends.

The LNWRS publications were inspiring and through the Society I met people who helped in many ways. I often say that until you start to make a model you don't realise what you don't know. When that happens, there is always somebody in the Society who can help and they have helped me enormously over many years.

Working in London I often attended auctions of model trains and was impressed by a large scale model by Bassett Lowke of an LNWR Experiment. How wonderful, I thought, to have one as a centrepiece in my railway room. John Hill offered me the mortal remains of such a model. I immediately ran a rule over it and found that in spite of being made in 1908, the model was dimensionally spot on for Gauge 3 - which I had never heard of. I joined the Gauge 3 Society and found that this really was a minority interest as no scale parts were available at all!

In 2000 my wife became ill and I was made redundant. I spent most of every day at the hospital until she died in December 2002. I was not feeling very sociable that Christmas, so on 25th December sat down on impulse to scratch build a model wagon in Gauge 3 to go with the Experiment. Well, I soon found that I rather liked this large scale where more detail could be included and I could see it!

I formed Williams Models and we have a range of 20 wagon kits, three carriages and three locomotives in development including a live steam LNWR 18in Goods.

To me the scale is perfect for detailed modelling but there is another side to it. I enjoy sitting in the garden on a summer's day beside a friend's track watching the trains go by. With Gauge 3 you not only watch them, but smell the steam and actually feel the vibrations and the heat from the boilers as they pass. That's what it must have been like standing beside the LNWR main line in its heyday!

Gauge 3 is one of the scales established before 1900 and was to a scale of ½in to the foot on a track gauge of 2.5in. In the late 1930s the scale changed to 17/32in/1ft, so that boilers could be larger and the change has stuck, being almost exactly 13.5mm/1ft. The gauge/scale ratio is also almost exactly correct and everybody works to the same scale and gauge - how refreshing!

In summary, I love modelling in Gauge 3 and would be really stuck without the help of the LNWRS and its members. My partner Denise is also a great support and physical help in many ways. I hope and believe that my father would have approved of these large models!

A Gauge 3 Diagram 12 timber wagon with dumb buffers, showing the level of detail that can be achieved at this scale. This was made from one of Mike's kits, the body being a one piece resin casting. It is sprung and the brake gear can be made to work! (Mike Williams)

Mike's first venture into Gauge 3 modelling, an LNWR Diagram 1 open goods wagon with 9 inch sides. Note the LNW diamond identification marks and wooden brake block. It has a resin body, laser cut W irons and brass sprung axleboxes. (Mike William

Surviving details of early LNWR rolling stock built prior to the 1870s are rather limited. Barry Lane made these 7mm scal model horseboxes back in the early 1980s based on measurements and details of some old grounded horsebox bodies. Som of the castings for the underframes came from Jim Richards. Note that there is no brake gear. The models won the Rollin Stock Cup at a Manchester Model Railway Society Exhibition in the 1980s.
The box on the left is a 14ft 3in long type. The model was based on the body of No 200 which was measured by Bill Ibbo just before it was destroyed. This vehicle had been built in November 1870. The horse box on the right is an earlier 13ft 6i long type built in the 1860s. It is believed that about 120 of the pre-14ft 6in horse boxes (a mix of 13ft 6in and 14ft 3in types were built and that they were all withdrawn in the 1890-94 period. It seems likely that there were detail design difference between vehicles and the 14ft 3in and 14ft 6in types may have been interchangeable to some extent. For further details o these early horse boxes, including some drawings, see *Journal* Volume 1 Numbers 5 and 10 and *Portfolio No 2*. (Barry Lane

FORTY YEAR OLD MODELS

These two signal box models were constructed about 40 years ago, one just before and one just after, the formation of the Society.

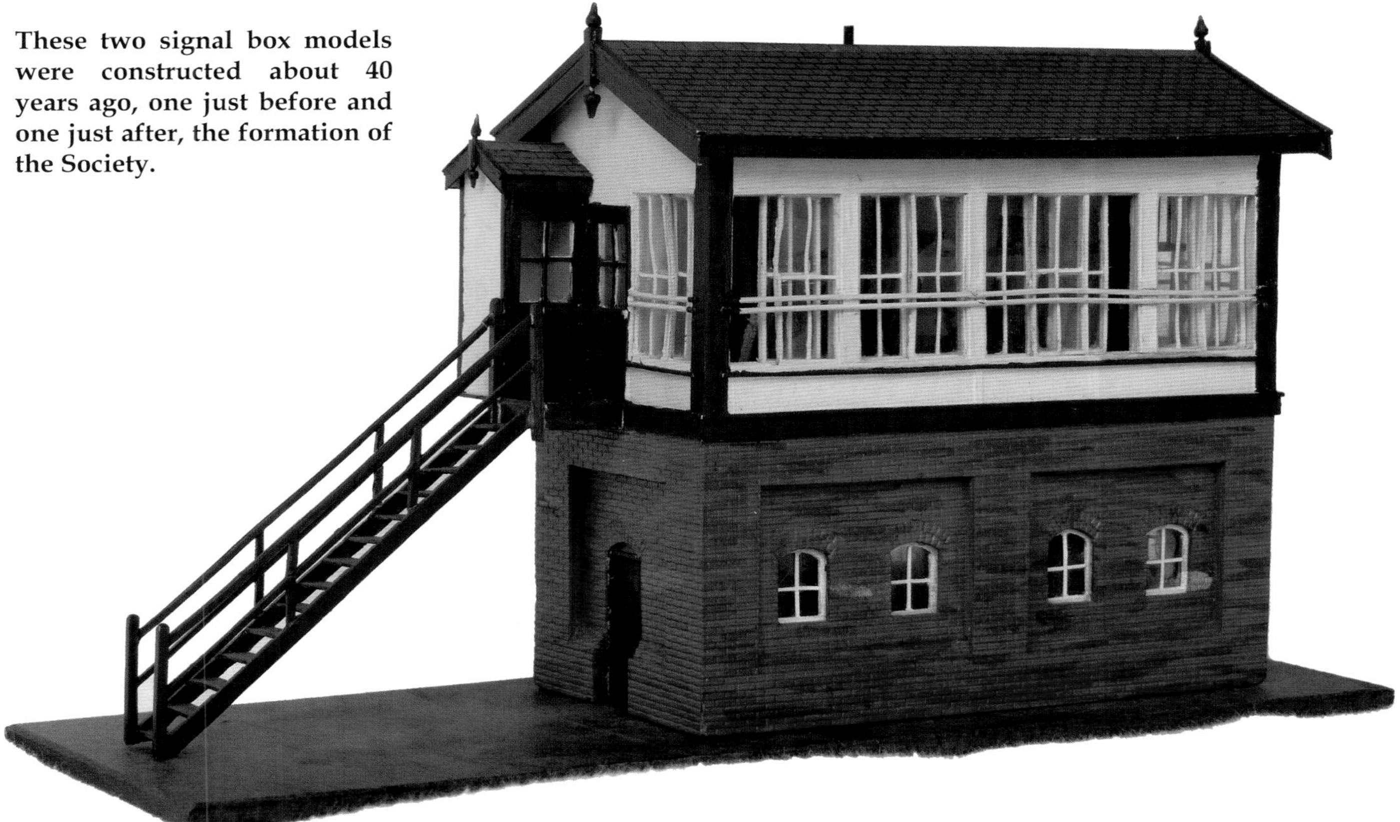

Richard Foster's model of a Type 5 signal box of size G, built to fill in Sundays while in digs doing work experience. The operating floor windows slide open or closed just as on the real thing! It won a Buchanan Award at the Manchester Model Railway Exhibition. The Plastikard has warped a little over the 40 years!

(Richard Foster)

Philip Millard's model of the impressive overhead Chester No 6 signal box. The real box opened in 1903, the box structure being 57ft 3in by 14ft, the extra width being useful in accommodating the 80 lever overhead type LNWR tumbler frame. Compare the metal structure on the box with the timber structure at Edge Hill No 1 (see the front cover).

(Philip Millard)

JACK NELSON AND JIM RICHARDS, AN

KINGSBURY
LIVERPOOL ROAD
LONDON & NORTH WESTERN
RAILWAY
COLLECTING VAN
FOR FAST TRAIN TRAFFIC
27
LNWR
London
Votes for
women

Nelson, John Kermeen – Jack or JK, F.I.S.T.C., Authority on the LNWR, Author of *LNWR Portrayed*, Constructor of Historic Models. Early Society Member. By Richard Foster

Jack Nelson was a man whose approach to recording the railway scene and to modelling was unique and both different to, and a long way ahead of, what was going on around him. As a result he has handed down to us a legacy which is still of immense lasting value.

Jack's father, John Nelson, was born in Ulpha, Dunnerdale, Cumberland, in 1872. He married Emma Kermeen (hence Jack's middle name), who was born in Waterloo, Liverpool in 1877, at St. Paul's Church, Kirkdale, in August 1906. John K Nelson (but always

With good wishes,
Yours sincerely,
Jack Nelson.

Signature from letter.

known as Jack) was born on 17th December 1909, when the family were living at Clare Road, Bootle. Also living there were John's mother, Agnes and his sister Dorothy. The 'railway' connection was established from the beginning, as the house was almost on top of Kirkdale tunnel on the L&YR Ormskirk line, and the LNWR Bootle branch was only about 100 yards away! John senior was a commercial clerk in a soap works, where his sister also worked. In 1913 the family moved to the Ilford area, but they made quite frequent visits to Liverpool to see their relatiives. It was those journeys from Euston which kindled Jack's love of the LNWR, and he found the industrial areas between Runcorn and Liverpool particularly fascinating!

While he dabbled a little with model railways as a child, as a teenager and young man he was, like many, fascinated by machines and speed. He made and flew model aircraft and had his own motorbike. Further education was at the South East Essex Technical College, followed by Kings College, University of London. During college days he became part-owner of a 'decrepit' motor boat, which he used while on family holidays in the Lake District.

Whitney Straight was a Grand Prix racing driver and flying enthusiast and owned or operated several airports, one of which was Margate, where, from about 1936, his company provided flying lessons and Jack learnt to fly with them.

Unfortunately many of his more physical activities had to be curtailed as a result of a very serious motorcycle accident he suffered in 1945. He was in a coma for several weeks and became acutely deaf. The accident also caused permanent damage to his right arm, and afterwards he only had quite limited use of the arm and hand and was told he would never write or draw again. He was having none of this and spent his convalescence learning to do these things! These limitations, when considered in the light of the drawings and modelling work he turned out during the remainder of his life, makes what he produced even more remarkable. When I watched the effort he had to put in to writing letters, notes and sketches it gave a tiny indication of the sheer effort and determination that went into all he produced.

His interest in railways began to return in the 1930s and research and modelling work got underway in earnest after his accident. Although the models usually had an LNWR theme, the scenes and non-railway buildings were largely imaginary. He tried to form a local model railway club, and as the majority of those interested were juniors, he formed the Ilford Junior Model Railway Club in 1945. This initially had its own premises, but they later met and built their models at Jack's home. In 1946 Jack, with a club member, visited, measured up and then made a model of Weedon station which was awarded prizes at an exhibition. The station later became the centre-piece in the club's layout. Many of his 1950s model magazine articles appeared under the club's name, notably his work in *Model Railway News,* the serious modeller's magazine of the period.

Jack became progressively more interested in depicting real railway scenes. He realised that the railways were changing and that what had been familiar to generations was being swept away. Something needed to be done to record some of the interesting railway scenes before they disappeared. He concluded that models provided an excellent way of bringing to life past scenes in a limited space, and began producing models of the buildings and scenes

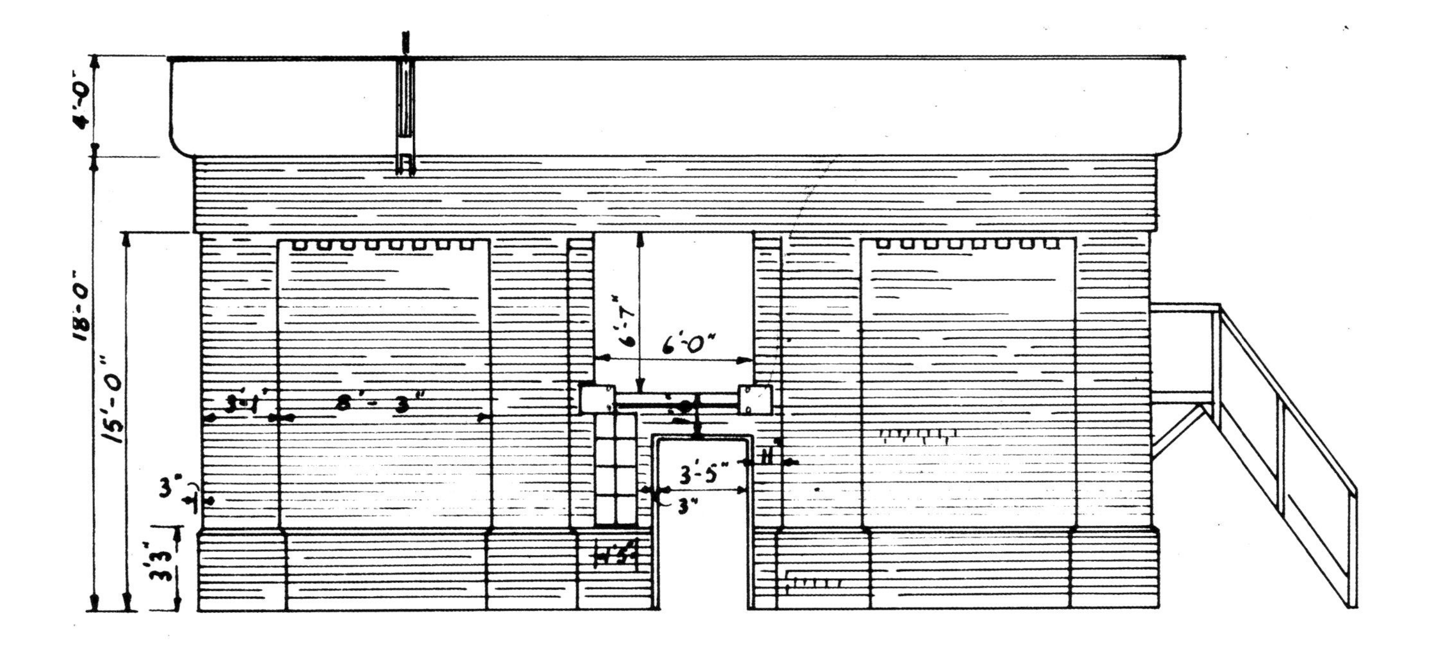

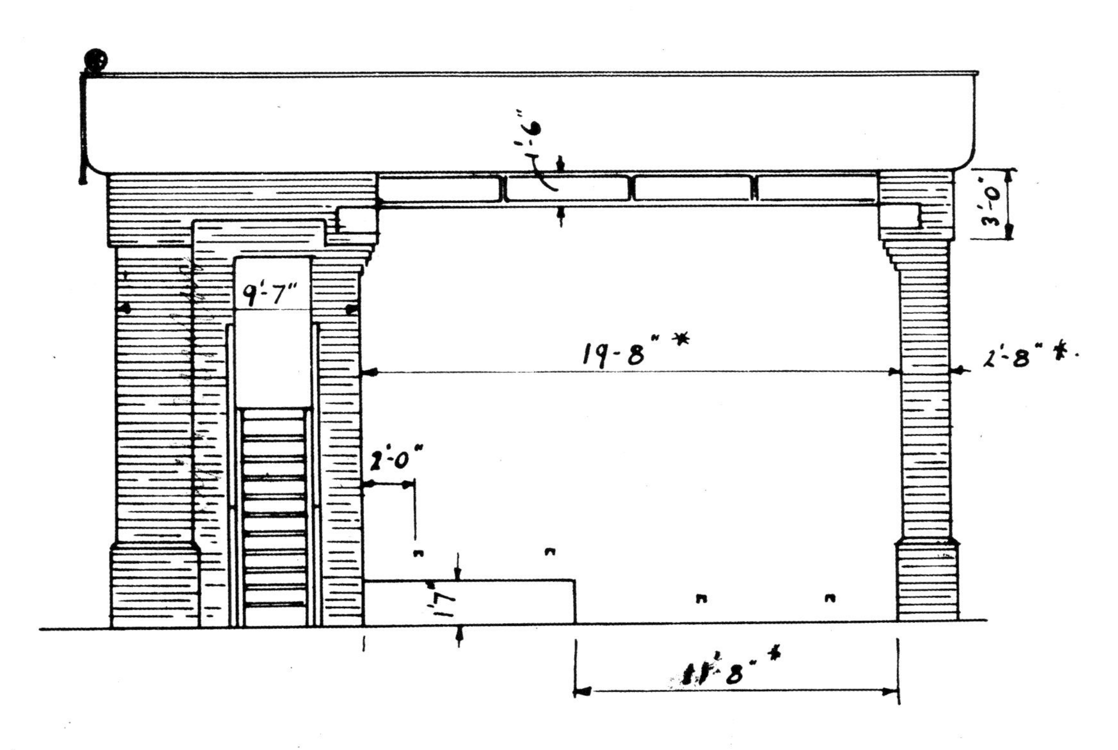

* DIMENSIONS FROM DUNN'S SKETCH MODIFIED AS DWN.
TO GIVE SUFFICIENT CLEARANCE FOR TWO ROADS.

An early drawing of Jack's done while he was convalescing from his accident, having been told he would never draw again! It is of the coal stage and water tower at Watford shed. The dimensions came from J M Dunn, but with the track opening altered for modelling purposes. This is a different structure to that in Figures 7.8 and 7.9 in *LNWR Portrayed*.

he knew. Many of the early models represented locations on his beloved Merseyside. He wanted accuracy, and initially worked to a scale of 3.5mm/ft with 00 gauge, but did some work in 7mm and ¾in/ft, adopting P4 standards for much of his later work.

His initial work was with conventional single scale models, but he quickly realised that even in quite small scales models representing large and complex areas took up a great deal of space and it was difficult to represent perspective and distances convincingly. He discovered that using progressively diminishing

Jack's sketch of an LNWR rotating ground signal done in the 1940s.

scales in layers would give greater depth to the rear parts of models. This was something Geoff Williams did with the backscene part of *Aylesbury*, and they would both have been aware of each other's work in developing these new techniques.

Jack began to think more about a comprehensive set of models to represent an LNWR route. One thought was to have continuous tracks where trains could run through a series of models showing particular scenes on the route. Each would appear as if in a separate display case as a 'snap-shot', so that the 'missing' sections would not be noticeable or jar. Naturally his thoughts turned to coverage of the London-Liverpool route. This might have started with a representation of a part of Euston station, followed by Camden bank with its burrowing junctions and electrically operated signalling, followed by the portals of Primrose Hill Tunnels and so on. Some models were made with this in mind, for example Runcorn and Widnes viaducts, and the coaling plant at Edge Hill. Even these snap-shot scenes took up a great deal of space.

On a visit to the South Kensington museums he saw perspective models or dioramas which allowed very large areas to be depicted in a very small space. The significant foreshortening was particularly effective for covering the long and thin nature of railways. He used this technique for his portrayal of Lime Street and Wavertree stations, which are illustrated, and remarked that the models were very enjoyable to build.

Studying the models is interesting. First it is evident that he must have had a very good eye and imagination to visualise what the model would look like, how the perspective worked, and the viewpoint needed to show what he wanted. He clearly knew what it would look like, as only the things that could be seen from the intended viewpoint were modelled in detail, while everything else was remarkably crude. As distance increased he also knew what could be modelled and painted as 'impressions' and how to get them to look right. It is also evident that cost was an issue for him, much being made from scraps and oddments. The dioramas are quite remarkable and repay detailed study, and are unique to Jack. It is these and the drawings which make him particularly special.

He thought that the models could form an attractive gallery in a museum. He contacted the museum in Liverpool and discussed his ideas with them, and they expressed interest. Unfortunately with personnel changes and financial restrictions they said that they were unlikely to be able to put together the 'Railway Gallery' that Jack had in mind. Thus in 1971 Jack tried a different tack, a note was published in the September *Railway Modeller* briefly describing what he had in mind, with a perspective sketch (it had to be!) of what a railway gallery might look like, and asking for help with the project and suggesting that a small group could probably achieve what was needed. The ideas were developed further and explained in more detail in *LNWR Portrayed*.

A Transport Trust was set up in Crewe with the idea of creating an LNWR based museum and for a time Jack hoped that they might be able to do what he wanted, and he donated the proceeds from the sale of his book to help them on their way. Eventually the National Railway Museum expressed interest and discussed the creation of the desired gallery and the models were moved there. Financial restrictions prevented any progress and the models were moved to the Conway Valley Railway Museum, where they can be viewed.

In preparation for his modelling work, Jack spent a lot of time photographing, measuring and drawing items of LNWR infrastructure, covering almost every aspect of the railway. This was in a period when access to railway information and drawings was limited, so he largely had to work from first principles. He

Jack Nelson's autograph in Richard Foster's copy of *LNWR Portrayed*.

put his personal mark on the work by producing many of the drawings in perspective form. Even in this he went a step further by producing some of the drawings in 'cut-away' form to show more clearly the construction details. Remembering the damaged arm and hand, this must have been slow and hard work, requiring considerable determination to keep going.

His drawing work bore fruit with the publication of his landmark book *LNWR Portrayed* by Peco Publications in 1975 and which featured over 300 of his superbly executed drawings, a work of dedication if ever there was one. The book and the models are particularly important as unfortunately it has not proved possible to trace his original drawings, while his photographic negatives were loaned out and never returned.

By profession Jack was a fellow of the Institute of Scientific and Technical Communicators. He was an active Christian and did a lot of work in the voluntary sector, most notably as a prison visitor and helping with prisoner rehabilitation pre- and post-release, work which spread over many years. He was a member of the Howard League for Penal Reform. His deafness was a considerable handicap when working with the people he met, particularly in the prisons, but he persevered.

In his later years Jack suffered increasing ill-health, and was eventually diagnosed with cancer, principally of the liver. By the time the problems were diagnosed, the cancer had spread too far to operate and after a spell in hospital, at his own request he was discharged so that he could spend his last days in his own home. Despite the fact that he was only able to

Jack's model of a busy city goods yard. This is probably an early model made before he began concentrating on depicting 'real' scenes. The delight of them is the amount of activity and detail depicted. Modelling goods yards and townscapes was pretty rare at the time, probably more or less contemporary with the pioneering work Geoff Williams was doing on *Aylesbury*. They certainly knew of each other's work. (John Mileson)

concentrate and stand for very short periods, he was still active in letter writing and offering information and advice up to a few days before his death. He died on 19th April 1979. His last letter to the Society was dated the 13th April and his last one to me a couple of days before he died.

Jack always kept in close contact with his sister, Margery, and after her first husband died, she went to live with him, and bore the brunt of caring for him as his illness developed. Jack was a long-time friend of John Skinley (they met at college), who is remembered for the large range of locomotive and rolling stock drawings he produced and sold commercially to help modellers during the 1950s, 60s and 70s. After Jack's death, Margery married John Skinley.

Above: Jack Nelson's model of Manchester Water Street. In the foreground is the bridge carrying the Manchester, South Junction and Altrincham Railway's Deansgate to Ordsall Lane link line over Water Street. The bridge in the distance is the original Liverpool and Manchester Railway bridge into Liverpool Road station. On the right, between the two bridges, is Liverpool Road with the stucco frontage of the original Liverpool & Manchester passenger station just visible on the right and the brick office building on the street corner. As with most of Jack's models, there is plenty of activity to make the scene interesting.

(John Mileson)

Jack Nelson's Christmas message to the Society in 1978:

'I have been asked to send a Christmas Message for *Premier News*. This I am happy to do as it gives me an opportunity at the same time to thank the officers and members who are doing much to further the interests of the Society. Good developments are on the way and the future is bright. I offer my sincere good wishes for Christmas and 1979.

(*PN25* Nov 1978)

Jack Nelson's Dioramas – The approach to Liverpool

One of Jack's particular specialisms was the creation of dioramas which allowed a large railway scene to be portrayed in a small space. He did two showing the approaches to Liverpool, and these are illustrated here, effectively creating an imaginary journey into Lime Street from the south around the 1910-20 period. These two pictures give a good impression of the effectiveness of this approach and of Jack's skills in getting the composition and perspective right, not at all easy to do from scratch.

The first model depicts Wavertree Station, looking north towards Lime Street and the Edge Hill yards. The view is looking along the down fast line. The signals are for Wavertree Junction, where trains could cross from fast to slow lines and vice versa. The main signals are 'off' for a train to Edge Hill and Lime Street and the passenger train can be seen in the distance, having just passed the signals. To its left is a southbound goods train which is just coming off the circular goods line and is heading onto the up slow. The other signals provided routes from the down fast to circular goods or the CLC goods depot. A southbound passenger train is in the up fast platform. Wavertree had wooden station buildings of the final design, nicely portrayed in perspective modelling. (John Mileson)

This view shows the station throat at Lime Street, looking from the signal box towards the station and buffer stops. The signal box was located between the up and down lines, so this is the up side. The track by the signal box is the station headshunt, that in the centre the up fast and the one on the right, with its separate tunnel, the up slow from platform 1. The big skew bridge carries Copperas Hill and the second bridge St. Vincent Street. As noted in the caption to the cover photograph it is of interest to wonder where Jack got the detailed information he would have needed to make this model. The signal box was removed and the trackwork extensively remodelled in 1948 and although he would have seen the area on his trips to Liverpool it is difficult to think he would have been able to remember the details sufficiently when he came to make the model about 15 years later. His lineside visit was presumably in the 1960s. (John Mileson)

Jim Richards in his workshop at Chirk. One can never forget the piercing blue eyes, full of life and interest.
(Courtesy National Railway Museum)

Richards, James Peel - Jim or JPR.

Authority on the LNWR, Supreme and Prolific Modeller, Prolific Correspondent, Society Member.

By Peter Davis, with additional material by Bob and Mike Williams and Richard Foster.

James Peel Richards, Jim to everyone, was the eldest son of Rupert Peel Richards. The 'Peel' in the family name came from their ancestor Sir Robert Peel, who had introduced the Police Force. Rupert was apprenticed to F W Webb at Crewe, about the same time as Nigel Gresley, afterwards working for Rendell, Palmer and Tritton. He left them in 1904 to take up the post of Works Manager of the *Vulcan Foundry* at Earlestown, becoming General Manager in 1917. Rupert bought Abergwynant Hall near Dolgellau around 1922, probably in anticipation of his retirement 1923, when he became a Director.

Jim was born on 8th March 1903, and was educated at Rugby School where he met sons of some LNWR officials including W E Dorrington (a Director). This appears to be when he started to take photographs of railway subjects (about 1919) - LNWR of course.

After school Jim became an apprentice at *Vulcan* studying engineering at Warrington Technical College during the evenings. In the Drawing Office, he produced the General Arrangement drawing for a batch of LMS compounds using only the old Midland Railway GA drawing, with alterations marked in red ink, which was all that the LMS had sent! As an LNWR enthusiast, he took the opportunity of copying *Vulcan*'s set of Crewe drawings of the 'G2' class 0-8-0 in his spare time.

In March 1926 he left *Vulcan* to join the *Crown Agents* as Inspector of Materials. He was based in Newport, Monmouthshire, when, during the General Strike, he did what all young men of his background did and volunteered for railway service. At Ebbw Junction shed he was paired with an ex-GWR driver, and together they had turns on 42XX and 45XX tank engines. Route learning seems not to have been a problem as they were told to ignore all signals except at junctions!

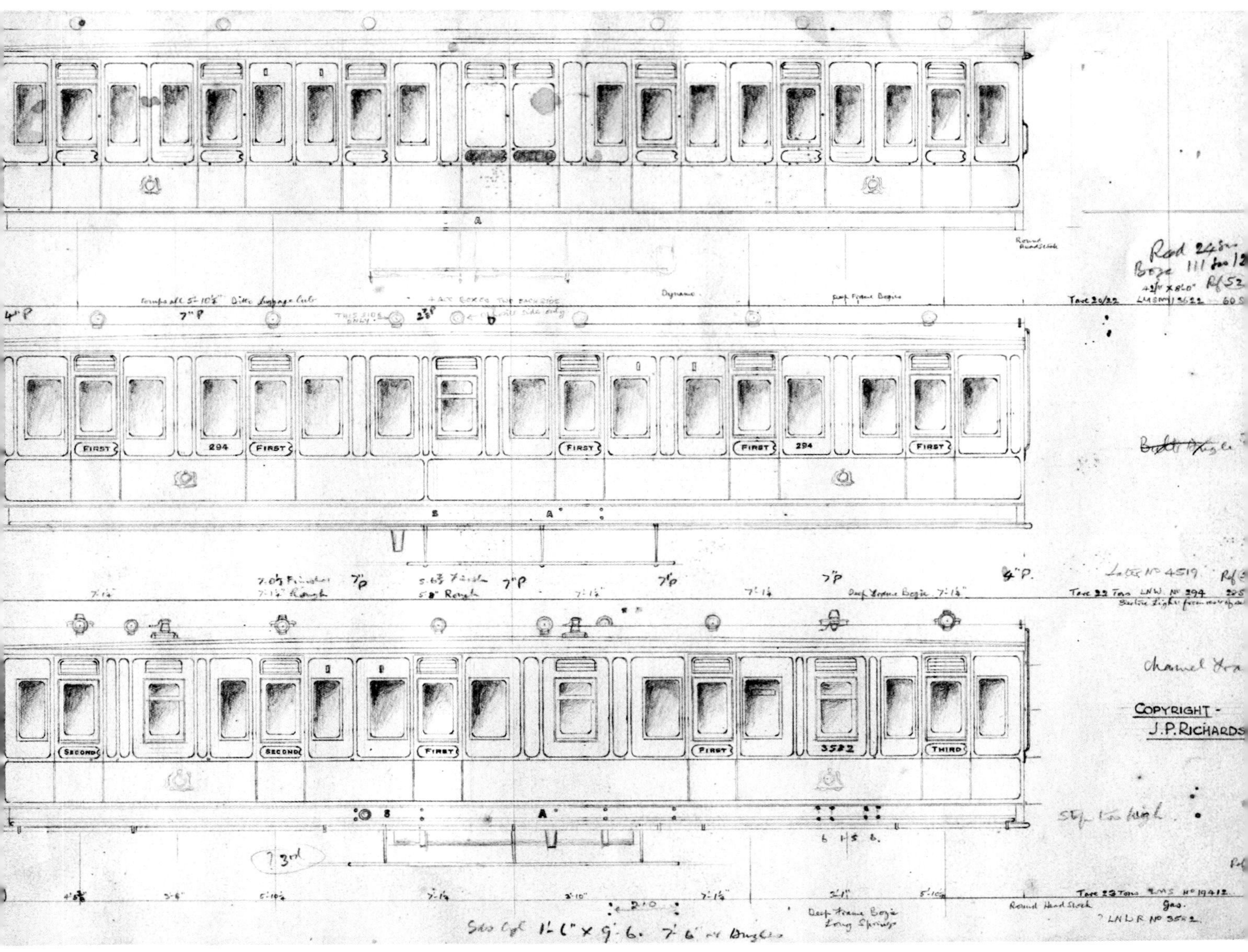

One of Jim's original carriage drawings, this one executed in pencil on cartridge paper.

The early thirties brought a change of direction. Abergwynant was sold and Jim and his younger brother Col took up farming near Southwater in Sussex. The family sold the Southwater Estate in 1946 and moved to Colwyn Bay, where Jim established himself as a model engineer, building model locomotives for several well-known customers and rebuilding most of W S Norris's engines when the latter altered his famous '0' gauge layout to fine scale. It was during this period that the patterns were made for the range of 7mm scale wagon axleguards and wheel castings that were marketed, together with the range of LNWR scale drawings, by *CCW Productions*. This material, and subsequent work by Jim, has formed the basis of practically all fine scale modelling of the LNWR, not just in '0' gauge.

Abergwynant was used by the Land Army during the war and some years later Jim bought it and in 1955 he moved the family back into their old home. The farms were not included in the sale, but a great swathe of the mountain was included. The place had been somewhat neglected, and one of the first jobs Jim and Col tackled was to rebuild the dam in the woods above the house and its leat to give increased head to the Pelton wheel from which they generated all of their own electricity.

It was only after the move to Abergwynant that Jim was able to commence serious work on his LNWR models. His life's ambition was to create a comprehensive set of models of LNWR trains, locomotives, carriages and wagons, together with a representative sample of the rolling stock of other companies that might be seen running over the LNWR. An important part of the plan was to create models of complete LNWR passenger trains he had seen running in his youth, and where he had either found information or meticulously recorded the details of all the vehicles he had seen on the train. Examples included a Birmingham-Euston train of 1910, a Manchester-Euston train from the 1906-19 period and a pre-electrification Watford set. Because of the huge number of vehicles he needed to make, he adopted mass-production techniques.

The first few years were spent in tool and pattern making and mass producing components ready to group into kits of parts. Most of the wagons had been built by 1970. The early seventies saw a move to carriages, while locomotive assembly got under way in earnest in the mid eighties. By this time he was in his eighties himself, but with no apparent regard for his age, he simply said 'I can get on with the locomotives now, I've only got 30 to do.' Such was the energy, dedication and generosity of this kindly man that, for a large proportion of the models he made, spare parts were made at the same time for 'other interested folk', as he put it.

As a trained locomotive engineer, Jim's expertise was valuable in the field of preservation. When J M Dunn's public appeal for funds to save the last Webb 'Coal Tank' fell largely on deaf ears, it was Jim who stumped up most of the purchase price and arranged for authentic fittings, like Webb buffers, to be included with the loco before it left Crewe. Similarly, his copies of the *Vulcan* 'G2' drawings, as well as his practical advice, proved invaluable to the National Railway Museum when they started to restore the 'Super D' 0-8-0.

Anyone who received a letter from Jim will appreciate the trouble he took to give accurate information in reply to queries; his lucid text was illustrated wherever appropriate with freehand drawings. Many who are now authorities on the LNWR received their grounding from Jim. Despite this, Jim was modest and self effacing to a degree; being something of a recluse, he never sought the limelight, seldom went to exhibitions or meetings let alone taking any part in the running of the many railway societies to which he belonged.

In 1982 Abergwynant was sold again and the family moved to Bryn Eglwys, near Chirk, in September, where the work on the models continued. Jim was diagnosed with cancer in 1997, but was determined, against all the odds, to complete his life's work. He almost finished the task when he died on 11th March, 1999, three days after his 96th birthday.

What made his collection of models unique was the consistently extreme high quality of the workmanship, combined with truly mind boggling quantity. Four hundred and fifty goods wagons, one hundred and sixty carriages and thirty locomotives, each as near perfect a model as is possible, is indeed a life's work. Nothing on this scale has ever been achieved before in the field of historical modelling and it is very doubtful that the feat will ever be equalled, let alone surpassed. The size of the collection led to an entry in the Guinness Book of Records. All the models are now at the National Railway Museum at York and are currently on display in the 'Warehouse' section.

Memories of Jim by Bill Allen (Former Society President)

Jim was devoted to the LNWR, but he was a model maker with a difference. He was supreme as a manipulator of metal; as skilled as a watchmaker in the handling of small parts for patterns, etc., and inventive in the design and construction of his rivetting machine. To see his models in operation was breathtaking. I believe Jim's work to be the best that has been constructed in 7mm scale up to this time.

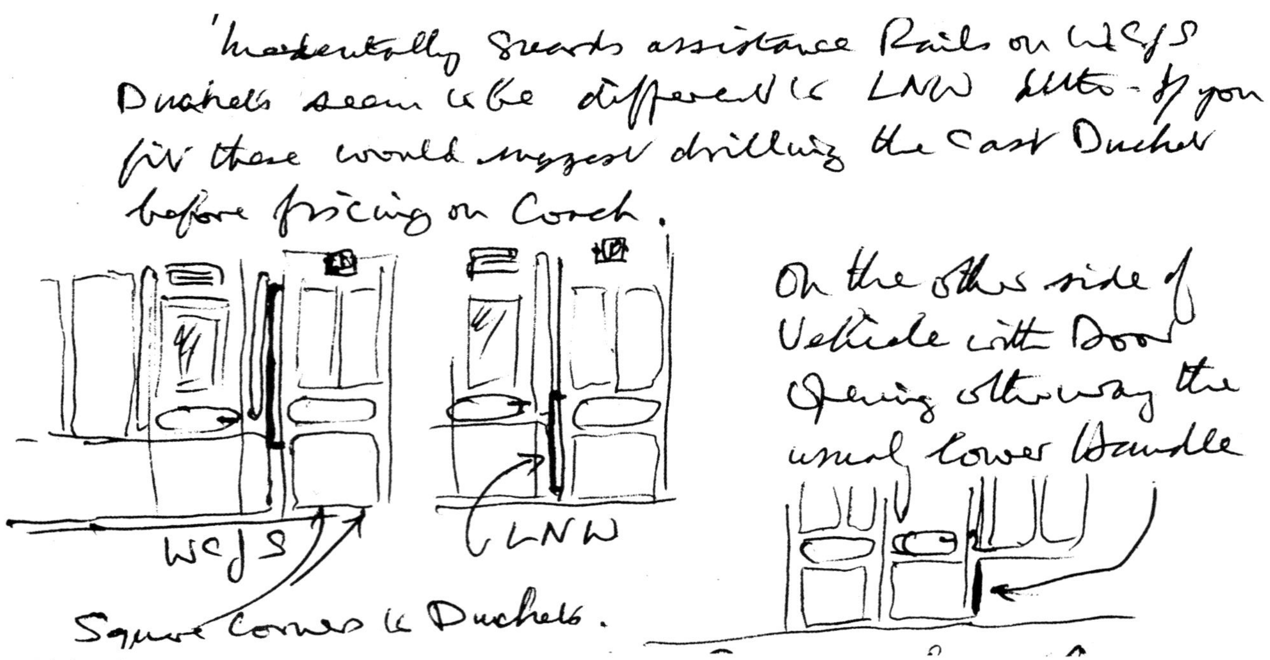

Jim Richards' letters often came with little sketches amongst the text to help explain a point. This example shows the differences Jim had found in the location of guard's 'assistance' handrails between WCJS and LNWR vehicles.

Memories of Jim by Bob Williams

Jim was particularly friendly with Geoff Platt, Arthur Gunn and F C (Bob) Hambleton. Jim described how they all used to go out together looking for interesting old railway relics to photograph and measure. All three were gentlemen in the true sense, authorities on their subjects, generous with their time helping fellow enthusiasts, and alas no longer with us.

Jim's production line approach and firm plan of what to build meant that he made all similar parts at once. Since few parts were available at that time he had to make everything himself and used Rocket Precision Ltd to cast them where necessary. Rocket were taken over by CCW, who had no idea what they had. Whitemetal castings were copied and copied without his approval, the quality deteriorating all the time. This he thought was a huge joke. For example, CCW listed 'DL1 and DL2 Diesel Louvers short and long'. In fact they were cast from Jim's patterns for LNWR 4-wheeled and 6-wheeled covered carriage trucks, but CCW never knew that! He was a pioneer in very many ways and adopted 33mm gauge decades before ScaleSeven existed.

Jim had a routine. He awoke early and dealt with correspondence, then went into the workshop for a full day's work. This continued into his 90s and because his workshop was so well equipped with ancient and home-made machines, he was able to turn out good quality parts and models even when he suffered from cataracts. He was also frugal to the extreme. On one occasion, sitting in his study, he reached for a scrap of paper on which to sketch some LNWR part, and pulled out an empty envelope which my father had send to him at least 20 years previously! All such things were always kept, just in case they were useful!

Jim Richards' model of a Diagram 42 wagon used for glass traffic from St. Helens. The wagon is modelled in its later form, as modified with a steel, rather than wood, well (Diagram 42A) which no doubt explains the higher tare weight than the original design. It includes a glass crate, complete with glass, and is a useful supplement to the illustrations in *LNWR Wagons Volume 1*, in showing what the crates looked like and how they were secured in position. (Courtesy National Railway Museum)

Jim Richards' model of a Diagram 84 10-ton open goods wagon loaded with cut timber. These wagons were 18 feet long and introduced in 1904 and 15000 had been built by 1921. This example has the short-lived single rib buffers and the final type of oil axleboxes, usually referred to as bulbous. It is in the post-1908 livery with both LNWR and diamonds. Compare the location of the '10 tons' inscription with the pictures in *LNWR Wagons*. Large quantities of cut timber in this form were imported through the LNWR's Garston Docks. The majority was loaded into open wagons as shown here, rather than onto timber wagons, for transit to destination.

(Courtesy National Railway Museum)

A Diagram 18 20-ton brake van labelled up for work between Crewe and Carlisle. The LNWR did not have many double-ended goods brake vans, but six of these were built for specific services. The model carries the livery of diamonds only, before the LNWR letters were introduced on wagons in 1908. It also, correctly, has buffers with 4-lugs and no ribs. The lamps are interesting. The tail lamp in the centre was mounted on a shelf inside the van so that it could be tended from the inside, with the light shining through a hole in the end wall. The red of the lamp can be seen. Later a hinged flap was provided at the end, giving access to lamp brackets which held the lamp outside. The side lamps are on hinged brackets so that they could be rotated out of sight when not in use or for attention. In addition to the bracket being hinged, the lamp itself can rotate on the bracket in order to present different colours for different purposes. Normally three red lamps were shown at the rear of goods trains, but where there were extra tracks, the following lights had to be shown to indicate to following trains which line the train was travelling on:

Four track sections, 3 red lights on the fast line, but when on the slow line a white light on the side nearest to the fast line
Loop lines adjacent to double track lines, a white light on the side nearest the main line.
Loop lines off four track lines, both side lamps to be removed.
Where brake vans were left in goods yards, guards were required to turn the sidelights inside before leaving the van.

(Courtesy National Railway Museum)

An LNWR steel-bodied gunpowder van to Diagram 43A. The GWR Iron Mink was adopted as the RCH standard for gunpowder traffic and the LNWR adapted the basic design. The doors were flush, rather than panelled as on the GWR design. Ten wagons of this design were built in the 1906-15 period. The colour these wagons were painted has been a source of discussion for many years. Bassett Lowke and Hornby both painted their contemporary models red but Ken Werrett, who claimed to have drawn all of his wagons from life, stated that they were grey. However a number of people claimed they were red. One writer said 'anyone who saw these vans can have no doubt that they were red'. The issue has never been satisfactorily resolved! Come what may, Jim chose the striking red colour, with post-1908 lettering. The inscription at the left-hand end reads 'To carry not more than 100 barrels, each barrel to weigh not more than 100 lbs'. This would give a maximum payload of about 4½ tons. (Courtesy National Railway Museum)

Jim Richards' model of a 10 ton Diagram 16 brake van. This was a very numerous type with 1465 built over the long period between about 1868 and 1901 and 288 of them passing to the LMS in 1923. They were 15ft 6in long by 7ft 6½in wide, on a short 8ft 6in wheelbase. The side lights were on swivel mounts and the tail lamp sat on an internal shelf with the light showing through a hole in the end wall. The example modelled had been allocated to the South Wales District.

(Courtesy National Railway Museum)

THE LNWR IN 1913 - ONE HUNDRED YEARS AGO

No 2222 *Sir Gilbert Claughton* when new, posed in photographic lined grey livery, January 1913.
(LNWRS LB Crewe Official B158)

While celebrating anniversaries, it is of interest to take a brief look at a few of the things that were happening on the LNWR a hundred years ago.

CLAUGHTON CLASS LOCOMOTIVES

Probably the most visually obvious event of 1913 was the introduction of C J Bowen Cooke's Claughton Class locomotives, the first of which, No 2222 *Sir Gilbert Claughton,* was turned out from Crewe Works in January. They had 4 cylinders, all driving onto the leading coupled axle, and a Belpaire firebox as used on the 4-6-2 Tanks. Rocking arms driven off the outside valve gear worked the inside valves in a similar manner to Webb's Jubilees (see the pictures of *Orion*). The *Daily Mail* stated that the engines cost approximately £5000 each. After extensive testing, *Sir Gilbert Claughton* had been put into regular service by June, normally working the 5.19pm Crewe-Carlisle and 1.0pm ex-Carlisle each day. On Sundays it worked the 5.5pm Crewe-Euston, returning with the 8.30am from Euston on Mondays. A further nine Claughtons were built during the year.

No 2222 *Sir Gilbert Claughton* now in working lined black livery and highly polished, posed at Wolverton with the carriages for the 10am Euston to Glasgow train. (LNWRS LB Crewe Official A589)

A modern 'Claughton' in miniature. This is Nigel Thompson's magnificent 5 inch gauge live steam model of 2222 *Sir Gilbert Claughton* posed at the Society Steam-Up in September 2004. Models like this are the nearest we can now get to what the locomotives looked like in three dimensions. (Ken Wood)

OPENING OF THE CENTRAL TIMING OFFICE

There were big changes in the way the LNWR compiled its working timetables in 1913. Up to then each Division and District was responsible for compiling its own working timetables and the associated engine, carriage and station working books and other working documents. Timetable staff were based in each District Superintendent's office to undertake the work. This system had existed from the early days and had grown with the railway. It had the advantages of local knowledge and control, but obvious weaknesses where trains crossed district boundaries, necessitating a lot of liaison. As traffic grew and traffic patterns became more complex these 'boundary' problems increased.

In 1912 the LNWR undertook a study into the working of the line and officers visited Derby to see what the Midland did. All their timetable work was done centrally in Derby and the officers were impressed by the comparative simplicity and efficiency of the operation. They decided that the LNWR needed a similar centralised timetable operation. Crewe, the hub of the system, was the obvious location. The new Central Timetable Office opened on Saturday 1st February 1913, located in temporary accommodation at the Mechanics Institute, pending completion of the construction of permanent offices at the station. Many of the divisional timetable staff were transferred to Crewe and from then on the main timetabling work for the whole railway was undertaken there. The compilation of the weekly engineering and operating notices was also transferred to Crewe and from 1st March the issue of notices was rationalised by combining those of several divisions into one. Compilation of the Public Timetable (the 'penny book') moved to Crewe on 1st January 1917 on the resignation of the departmental chief.

A comprehensive article on the Central Timing Office and the timetabling work appeared in the June 2013 issue of the *Journal* (Vol 7 No 5).

The train controller's office and control board at Bescot Control Office, which opened in December 1912, (not quite 1913, but near enough!) It is assumed that all the LNWR control offices had boards like this and were laid out in the same way. On each of the desks is a 24-way telephone circuit board with key switches, giving direct communication with the main signal boxes and traffic centres in the district. The board had a representation of the railway network in the control area showing the running lines, loops and yards. There were sockets adjacent to signal boxes, loops and yards into which pegs could be put to show the positions of trains. The assistant controllers were required to keep this up to date.

TRAIN CONTROL OFFICES

Strictly this was a 1912 innovation, but the bulk of the implementation was undertaken in 1913. While the working timetables, train marshalling books and other working instructions provided a framework for working the traffic, they could not cover variations in traffic, special traffics, delays and disruptions and other issues. The people on the ground had to manage as best they could, but it was easy for one person's decisions to adversely affect another's. The Midland introduced a 'Control Office' at Masborough in 1907-8 where a dedicated set of staff could have an overview of a whole area with direct communication to signal boxes, yards and stations. With the 'big picture' available they could make the best decisions to sort out problems and inform everyone. The trial was very successful and was soon extended.

The LNWR undertook some trials with the regulation (or control) of engine working in 1910, and after the review of the working of the line in 1912, established a Train Regulators' Office at Rugby in September 1912. Following the success of this operation, the scheme was extended, with a Control Office opening at Bescot in December. The bulk of the scheme was implemented in 1913 when a series of new Control or Regulators' Offices were opened:

January	Huddersfield;
February	Nuneaton;
April	Heaton Norris and Warrington;
May	Springs Branch and Preston;
June	Patricroft and Willesden;
September	Bletchley, Shrewsbury and Basford Hall;
November	Edge Hill.

Each office generally consisted of three rooms, the Chief Controller's Office, the control room and a telephone test room. In most cases there were three controllers on duty on each shift. The Head Controller was responsible for the overall management of the traffic in the district. The Assistant Traffic Controller received telephone messages, obtained information on the working of the traffic and kept the control board up to date. He was assisted by the Assistant Locomotive Controller who kept them all up to date with motive power issues. He also dealt with the relief arrangements for enginemen and guards.

The control system was further extended in subsequent years. Train control is still a vital part of railway operations today.

ROYAL VISITS

1913 was a busy time for Royal visits, with King George V and Queen Mary making tours of the North West, involving extensive use of the LNWR Royal Train with travel over LNWR and L&YR routes. Crewe and the Potteries were visited in April and Lancashire in July. In preparation, the LNWR Royal Train made a trial run from Wolverton to Crewe and into the Works on 27th February, returning via Platform 4 at Crewe Station, which was the one the Royal couple used to rejoin the train after their four-day Potteries tour.

On 21st April the Royal party travelled to Crewe for a visit to Crewe Locomotive Works. Frederick Manning, the Mayor of Crewe, met their Majesties on the arrival of the Royal Train at Crewe Station at 2.28pm (two minutes early!) and presented them with an Address on behalf of the Town. Manning was a signalman at Basford Hall Junction signal box. He was Mayor for 1913, and Liberal by politics. Prior to his appointment he had obtained permission from the LNWR to alter his shifts or take leave of absence so that he would be able to undertake his civic duties. The Address itself was the work of Mr J H R Fisher, Chief Clerk at the Old Works Time Office.

The Royal Train was 'equal to 18½' and worked by engine 5000 *Coronation*, with 2663 *George the Fifth* attached. C J Bowen Cooke showed the Royal couple around the Works, with internal transport by means of two of the Works cabs, the visit taking just under 1½ hours. The King knighted Robert Turnbull, Superintendent of the Line, that evening. Also that evening the LNWR held a reception for 400 guests in the Works Drawing Office, at which, among others, Manning spoke, and Sir Frank Ree said that the Company proposed to put a commemorative tablet in Basford Hall signal box. At the end of his year of office a banquet was held in honour of Manning, at which a number of senior LNWR officials were present, including Sir Gilbert Claughton, the Company Chairman, and Bowen Cooke.

After visiting Crewe Works, the King and Queen were driven through the town on their way to Crewe Hall where they spent three nights as guests of the Marquis of Crewe. The Hall provided a base for their visits to the Potteries.

In July there was an extensive 8-day tour of Lancashire, the Royal Train leaving Euston on Monday 7th July for Warrington. The tour included visits to Preston, Lytham and Blackpool on the 8th, Blackburn on the 10th, a visit to Horwich Works and finished in Manchester and Salford on the 14th.

The brass plaque in Basford Hall Junction Signal Box which commemorates the Royal Visit in 1913. The text reads:

'This tablet commemorates the visit of Their Majesties King George V and Queen Mary to Crewe Works on April 21st 1913, Frederick Manning, a signalman in charge of this box, being Mayor of Crewe. On behalf of his fellow townsmen he received Their Majesties and presented them with an address on their arrival at Crewe Station.'

Crewe Old Works Yard. Queen Mary, with her magnificent hat, and King George near the end of their visit. The gentleman beyond the Queen, on the left, is Sir Gilbert Claughton , the Chairman of the LNWR.

(LNWRS RVC60)

Frederick Manning, LNWR signalman at Basford Hall Signal Box in his gown and chain at the start of his term of office as Mayor of Crewe for 1913.

LNWR STATISTICS

In connection with the Royal Visit to Crewe, the LNWR published the following statistics on the Company and its activities:

Capital	£ 116,188,591
Revenue per annum	£ 16,733,193
Expenditure per annum	£ 10,885,041
Miles operated on	3,038
Miles owned, partly owned or leased	2,063
Miles of Canals	114
Passengers carried (excluding season tickets)	79,005,445
Season tickets issued	184,327
Tons of goods and minerals carried	54,517,214
Engine miles	76,327,262
Number of persons employed by the Company	86,500
Number of persons employed in the locomotive department	20,683
Number of stations	800
Number of signal cabins	1,294
Number of signal levers in use	38,112
Engines owned, including rail motors	3,111
Carriages owned	9,216
Wagons owned	78,450
Carts owned	7,107
Horses owned	6,086
Steamships owned	16

New Works

Completed in 1913 was the section of the Watford 'New' line between Harrow and Watford, 5¾ miles. Widening works in progress were between Nuneaton and Atherstone, Armitage and Rugeley and at Lichfield Trent Valley.

New stations opened for passengers were:

Burlington Road Halt (P&W)	1 October 1913
Garn-yr-Erw Halt	1 February 1913
Gillett's Crossing (P&W)	1 October 1913
Headstone Lane	10 February 1913

Capital expenditure for 1913 was £ 839,310

THE LONDON & NORTH WESTERN RAILWAY SOCIETY – THE FIRST FORTY YEARS.

BY RICHARD FOSTER

It often seems that when railway anniversaries are celebrated, there has to be a picture of a locomotive bearing that number, so here it is! This is 'Precursor' 40 *Niagara*, which was built in March 1905, Crewe Works Number 4470. It became LMS 5198 in January 1928 and was withdrawn in November 1930. In fact this was the 5th No 40 on the LNWR. The number had been applied to a Grand Junction engine of 1846, a passenger engine of 1847, to *Raven*, a 7ft passenger engine of 1857 and a Coal Engine of 1876. (Photo Collection SOC 1304)

ORIGINS OF THE SOCIETY

The first attempt to set up a society for those interested in the London & North Western Railway was as far back as 1962. In those days there were the 'national' railway societies, covering all companies and areas, a few local societies providing local meetings and just a tiny handful of pioneering line or regionally-based societies. For those interested in locomotives the obvious one to join was the Stephenson Locomotive Society, whose *Journal* featured many articles on the LNWR over the years, notably a list of Crewe-built locomotives based on the notes of S S Scott, published in parts from 1953 to 1958, but sadly never completed. Many of the pioneer names in LNWR history, and early members of our Society, can be found in the SLS membership lists. For other areas of historical interest, the choice was either the Historical Model Railway Society or the Railway & Canal Historical Society.

In 1962 letters and notes appeared suggesting the formation of a society to further knowledge and interest in the LNWR and advertising a meeting to consider the formation of a society. This meeting took place at Central Station, Manchester, on 15th September 1962, where it was decided to set up the London & North Western Railway Historical Society to 'further the knowledge and historical study of that railway'. The subscription was set at 10 shillings and 6 pence, or free to ex-LNWR employees. The instigator of the proposal seems to have been our own G Dudley Whitworth. Dudley became chairman and Bertram Baxter the Treasurer.

The initial membership list contained twenty-five names, many well-known to us and in writings on LNWR matters. These included: **Bertram Baxter,** of the *British Locomotive Catalogue 1825 to 1923.* His life's work was the listing of locomotives and by the time of his death he had built up a card index of some 46,000 items; **J M Dunn** of *Reflections on a Railway Career LNWR to BR* (1966) and largely responsible for the preservation of the LNWR Coal Tank (I loved the title of an article he once wrote: *I bought a Locomotive*); **Neil Fraser**; **Jack Nelson; G H Platt; D H Stuart,** one of the last LNWR Pupils under Beames, and co-author of *The Crewe Type* (1971) which for the first time gave us the true history of Crewe's earliest locomotives; and finally a youthful **Harry Jack,** an LNWRS member to this day and a former Society President!

The LNWRHS produced several typescript newsletters. *Bulletin* (as it was titled) *No 1* was published in January 1963. It noted that C Williams of Crewe had consented to become the society president - a father figure indeed. Williams of course was *the* supreme authority on the complexities of LNWR engine numbering, having published several books of lists from 1907 to 1924. His regular LNWR and LMS contributions to the *Railway Magazine* as 'Our Crewe Correspondent' ran for about sixty years. That he had agreed was quite an endorsement for the embryonic society. A complete reprint of the contents of *Bulletin No 1* was included in our Portfolio No 9 - *LNWR One Man's Passion - A Tribute to G D Whitworth*, published in 1991.

Bulletin No 2 followed in April 1963, when membership had reached sixty, a rather impressive number. It again consisted of four duplicated pages and included articles on 'Engine Drivers & their Work', reprinted from the *Strand Magazine* 1894, and Grand Junction Locomotives 1841 & 1842, by C H Codling. *Bulletin No 3* did not appear until March 1964, and was prefaced by the following;

'It is eleven months since the previous *Bulletin* came out. This is regrettable, particularly so, because there has been no flow of information suitable for inclusion in our pages.'

Editors having to appeal for material for publication is evidently a perennial problem for societies! Income from subscriptions in 1963 was £34 10s 6d and expenditure was just £3 10s 6d including the issue of two *Bulletins*. There was a note that the Coal Tank was now at Penrhyn Castle Museum, and of J M Dunn's part in its preservation. Most intriguing, there was the following note:

PORTFOLIOS. A start has been made with compiling small portfolios on various subjects. It is intended that these will circulate among our members, who may retain them for a fortnight before returning them to the committee. The subjects to date are:

No 1 The Oldham Ashton & Guide Bridge Junction Rly by N Fraser

No 2 Normanton, An outpost of the LNWR by N Fraser

No 3 Grand Junction Loco List 1837 to 1846 by H Finch

No 4 Amended Notice. LNWR South Wales Division Coal Strike, 1912

No 5 The Sirhowy Plate Way & Railway, various notes.

(Does anyone have copies of any of these?)

Bulletin No.4 appeared in January 1965, most of which was taken up with the first part of a detailed numerical list of LNWR locomotives (Nos. 1 to 36). However, it would seem that no further *Bulletins* were ever produced. The only other note from the historical society I have found is a notice dated 29th December 1966, for a meeting on 14th January 1967. This records the death of Bertram Baxter in October 1966. After this the society seems to have become moribund. There matters seem to have rested for nearly 10 years.

FORMATION OF THE LNWR SOCIETY

Eric Rayner, of Stockport, posted a notice at the Manchester Model Railway Exhibition in December 1972 asking those interested in forming a society to promote the memory of the LNWR to contact him. He arranged a meeting at Crewe Library on 7th July 1973 for interested people to discuss options and proposals to form an LNWR Society.

Eric was a life-long LNWR enthusiast, but long-term illness limited his activities. His object in trying to start the society was to bring together people with similar interests, and particularly those with knowledge which could then be disseminated through the society so that everyone would learn and there would be mechanisms for finding new information and spreading the products of research.

Eric took along Robert 'Robbo' Ormiston-Chant to help him run the meeting and record events. The meeting was attended by twenty-three people and decided that a society should be formed. A proposal that it should be called the 'London & North Western Railway Society' was voted on, and carried by 22 votes to 1. The meeting considered the society's objectives. After discussion, a resolution was put forward by Mr T W 'Smokey' Bourne of Halesowen, a well-known modeller and LMS Society member, and seconded by Eric Rayner, that:

'The objects of the Society are to preserve the memory of and to publicise the activities of the London & North Western Railway Company.'

Once again the vote was 22 for and 1 against.

When it came to considering a constitution and rules, one of the people present, Mr J C James of Liverpool, put forward a ready-made constitution and rules and attempted to get these agreed. These were considered by the meeting to be unsuitable and that simpler alternatives were available. A probable issue was that the majority of the people present wished the Society to be a historical one, whereas Mr James's main interest was in preservation.

The following volunteered to form a 'steering committee' to take on setting up the Society and administer its affairs and were accepted by unanimous consent:

E Rayner, R C Ormiston-Chant, C S Taylor,

J G Thomas, P J Thomas, G D Whitworth and

B A Yarnold.

Following the main meeting the steering committee met and adopted Eric Rayner as Chairman, Robbo Ormiston-Chant as Secretary, and Dudley Whitworth as Treasurer. I was not at this first meeting, but seem to have heard about the Society shortly after it took place and contacted Eric direct, arranging to visit him on 28th July.

The first formal meeting of the Society was held on 29th September 1973, again in Crewe library. Attendance was again twenty-three people present as at the first meeting, although not all were the same people. When the question of a committee came up, those from the first meeting indicated they were prepared to continue and further volunteers from the floor were requested. Although I had not been at the first meeting, in a moment of weakness I put myself forward, and thus began my 40 year association with the running of the Society. This enlarged 'committee' group was accepted unanimously.

The issue of constitution and rules was considered in detail and a final form of each rule agreed. Then came the often controversial subject of subscriptions, and proposals for £2 and £3 were put forward. Votes were 12 for £3, and 9 for £2. There was debate about the form of publications and communications with members. Mike Peascod suggested a newsletter and data sheets on specific subjects which could be distributed and offered for sale. The first became *LNWRS News* and the second *Premier Pamphlets*. A feature of the meeting was discussions on arrangements for a Society badge, something many members of societies seemed to find important at that period, but which seems to have now gone completely out of fashion.

The formation of the Society was announced with a paragraph in *The Railway Magazine* for February 1974:

'London & North Western Railway Society

Formed at a recent meeting in Crewe, the London & North Western Railway Society has been inaugurated to preserve the memory and publicise the activities of the old London & North Western Railway, particularly becoming a clearing house for information of all kinds about the LNWR. The Hon. Secretary of the Steering Committee of the Society is R. C. Ormiston-Chant, 17 Roseleigh Avenue, Manchester, M19 2NP. The Society is not connected with the London & North Western Society, formerly the LNWR Coaching Stock Fund (*RM* November 1973 p589).'

The second general meeting of the Society was held at Crewe library on 30th March 1974. The treasurer reported a subscription income of £147, presumably indicating a total membership of 49, with total funds before expenses of £184. An intriguing feature of the accounts was a £30.86 'Inheritance' from the long-defunct LNWR Historical Society. Presumably Dudley Whitworth had carefully kept the money safe over the intervening years!

The greatest difficulty the Society faced over the first two years was the lack of an editor and 'Robbo' Ormiston-Chant tried to combine the work of secretary and editor. 'Robbo' was somewhat disorganised and things tended to happen by fits and starts and not always coherently. Some of the newsletters looked as if he had suddenly realised that one was overdue, so had sat down and typed the first things that came to hand! After three issues of *LNWRS News*, the title mysteriously changed to *Premier News* at the beginning of 1974, with the number series starting again from 1. The editorial and administrative problems, and the presence of another group with a similar name, unfortunately rather inhibited the growth of the Society over the first few years.

ANOTHER LNW SOCIETY

Sometime in the late 1960s an 'LNWR Coaching Stock Fund' had been set up to save, purchase and restore some ex-LNWR carriages about to be scrapped by British Railways. A couple of vehicles, a 50ft arc-roof full brake and a 57ft suburban third, were saved and moved to the then Railway Preservation Society site at Hednesford (later Chasewater). The first of these vehicles was used for many years for a display of small LNWR relics. Both are still at Chasewater in poor condition.

Mr J C James was one of the main people involved with this organisation and it was he who put the 'ready-made' constitution forward at this Society's inaugural meeting and was the dissenting voice in some of the resolutions voted on at that meeting.

Shortly after the LNWRS inaugural meeting in July 1973 the Coaching Stock Fund reorganised and reconstituted itself, changing its name to the London & North Western Society (no 'Railway'), the change being recorded in *The Railway Magazine* for November 1973:

'LNWR Fund Becomes Society

The LNWR Coaching Stock Fund as founded has been reorganised and re-constituted as the London & North Western Society. New entrants will pay an entrance fee of 50p plus an annual subscription of 50p, with a minimum age limit of 12 years. Enquiries should be addressed to Mr J C James, Solaby, 4 Longview Drive, Huyton, Liverpool, L36 6EE.'

To anyone seeing the notes on the two societies in the magazines there was no real way of telling what the differences between the two were. The LNW Society advertised a meeting in Liverpool on 19th January 1974, and this was attended by two of our own long-standing members, Harry Jack and Huw Edwards. Huw found and joined the LNWRS in March 1974 and Harry in May 1976. The similarities of the two society names caused some confusion among external organisations and people, and the committee members had to spend a fair amount of time explaining the situation and sorting out misunderstandings.

OUR FIRST SPEAKER

The September 1974 meeting was something of a landmark, being the first meeting at which a speaker had been invited to give a talk to members. This was none other than Geoffrey H Platt, one of the great experts on the LNWR, and very much a father figure for what the Society wanted to achieve. At this time he was Chairman of the Historical Model Railway Society. Very much the case of starting as we meant to go on - with the best!

1975 - A YEAR OF CHANGE AND DEVELOPMENT

In 1975 things began to change and develop for the better. First, Graham Thomas, one of the original steering committee members, agreed to take over as Secretary. Eric Rayner had to reluctantly accept that his bouts of illness made it impossible for him to carry out the work of Chairman and said he wished to resign. This was considered at the AGM in March and, in the absence of any other volunteers, I was elected to take on the role of Chairman. I seem to recall that this followed considerable encouragement (= pressure!) from 'Smokey' Bourne, although the formal proposal was put by David Clarke and Brian Metcalfe; I had already stood in for Eric on several occasions. By unanimous vote Eric was elected the Society's first President, following a proposal from 'Smokey'.

This left the problem of the editorship. Fortunately a new character appeared on the scene in the form of the dynamic David Clarke, who we managed to persuade to join the Committee and take on the role of Editor, which he did from the seventh issue of *Premier News* in July 1975. Mike Bland also stepped in to act as the Society's first Photographic Officer, although not initially a committee member.

David Clarke was also a keen modeller, and ran the 'Modelling Section' of the Society for a number of years, publishing a great deal of modelling information. The quality of the material sent to members through *Premier News* and other publications progressively improved. The cost of printing for small quantities was prohibitive in those days and the copy for anything the Society sent to members had to be painstakingly typed onto stencils and then duplicated on a duplicating machine. A step forward was the purchase in 1974 of a second-hand hand-operated Roneo duplicating machine, a big step at the time, bearing in mind that the Society's total income was less than £200 a year! More work for the editor of course. Once he had finished typing he had to load the machine and stand there cranking until there were copies of everything for all the members. Despite this, David Clarke also found time to arrange Society stands at some model railway exhibitions in the North-West.

September 1975 saw the issue of the first special single-subject publication, *Premier Pamphlet – 'Non-Passenger Coaching Stock'* by T W Bourne (3 duplicated pages). This set the pattern for the Society's regular printed offerings to members through to 1981, following the pattern suggested at the September 1973 meeting. The core was *Premier News* containing Society news and administrative matters and small items relating to the LNWR. This was supplemented by several series. First, a *Modelling Supplement* containing information on new models and availability, happenings in the trade and events. One was issued with almost every *PN* during David Clarke's period as Editor. Next a series *Odds and Ends* containing snippets of information and short articles on the LNWR, and last, but by no means least, papers on specific subjects, the equivalent of today's *Journal* articles. The latter built up into quite a sizable collection of LNWR information over the years. Initially *Premier News* and its supplements were intended to be issued 6 times a year, but in some years only 4 or 5 were produced.

A further development in 1975 was the introduction of a drawings service, offering prints from drawings or microfilms. 1976 saw the Society try its first exhibition, open to all, with a 2-day event at Crewe Grammar School. The centre-piece was naturally the Rugeley model layout belonging to Brian Metcalf and the School. This was supplemented by some of Geoff Platt's magnificent 0 gauge models, a huge selection of LNWR cast-iron signs and photograph displays. Unfortunately there were only 12 members among the visitors (judging member interest for events and estimating likely attendances is one of our eternal problems), although these did include Jack Nelson. New members joining in 1976 included Harry Jack, Dave Pennington and David Patrick, while Mike Bland and Roy Thomson joined the Committee.

1976 TO 1990

Outside the Society, 1976 was notable for the operation of *Hardwicke* on a number of special passenger trains. May was the 100th Anniversary of the opening of the Midland's Settle & Carlisle line, and special trains were arranged with steam haulage from Carnforth to Hellifield. The rostered locomotive was the Midland Compound, but this developed problems and on the day the trains were hauled by *Hardwicke* and *Flying Scotsman*! An LNWR engine marking the Centenary of a Midland line! On 9th May *Hardwicke* operated a shuttle service of trains between Carnforth and Grange-over-Sands on its own, looking quite small against the four Mark 1 coaches. Members travelling included Dudley Whitworth, Bill Finch, David Clarke and Richard Foster. On 19th June, *Hardwicke* and *Evening Star* double-headed a 13 coach train from Carnforth to York; talk about David and Goliath!

At the April 1978 AGM Sandy Croall replaced Graham Thomas as Secretary. In the summer Jack Nelson accepted our invitation to become President of the Society, with Bill Allen taking up the position in the summer of 1979, Patrick Fisher in 1980 and Dudley Whitworth in 1981.

The Society's first booklet or *Premier Publication* covering the Friezeland accident of 1909 came in 1977. It cost the Society £42 to produce, 20 percent of the Society's income at the time! It set the general policy of issuing the special publications free to members wherever possible.

The Society Library started in a small way in 1980, with Mike Warren as Librarian. Mike stepped down in 1982 and Dave Pennington took on the role. Dave is now by far the Society's longest-serving officer, still going strong 31 years later!

Carnforth station on 9th May 1976 with 790 *Hardwicke* at the head of one of the trains which it operated between there and Grange-over-Sands. As can be seen, the trains were very popular. The little loco 'jumped about' noticeably when travelling at speed at the head of the trains. This loco had an eventful start to its life. It was turned out from Crewe in April 1892, and on 27th May it was involved in an accident at Derby Junction, Birmingham, as a result of which it fell off Lawley Street viaduct into a yard below. Crewe locos were made of stern stuff, so it was returned to traffic after repair and is still with us! (Richard Foster)

The big external event of 1980 was the celebration of the 150th Anniversary of the opening of the Liverpool and Manchester Railway with a festival, exhibitions and re-enactments of the cavalcades of 1930 under the title 'Rail 150'. The Society was represented with a stand, exhibits and photographs. Fortunately Colin Reed, who had recently joined the Committee, took on the task of organising things. Member Aidin Hull paid the costs of the Society stand and loaned the majority of the exhibits, afterwards donating some of the material to the Library.

1980 and 1981 brought changes on the Committee. Clive Taylor replaced David Clarke as Editor and Sandy Croall relinquished the Secretary role and Geoff Williams became Secretary from May 1981. Dudley Whitworth, Treasurer since the formation of the Society, stepped down at the same time, being elected Society President in recognition of his contribution to the Society and his huge knowledge of the LNWR. Roy Thomson took on the Treasurer role.

The late 1970s and early 1980s were rather a traumatic period with the loss of several 'elder statesmen' members. Eric Rayner, our founder, died following a heart attack in March 1978; Jack Nelson died of cancer in April 1979; and Geoff Platt died from a heart attack in July 1980.

Dudley Whitworth, another 'elder statesman' who had contributed so much to the Society, died in July 1988. There were significant changes to the Committee that year. After 13 years as Chairman I stepped down and was replaced by Roy Thomson, and Geoff Williams also stepped down as Secretary, being replaced by Andy Lowe. Denis Nix had replaced Roy Thomson as Treasurer the previous year. Norman Lee took over from Mike Bland as Photographic Officer, a post he still holds today, being our second-longest serving officer after Dave Pennington. I was elected Society President at the AGM in May 1988.

The year 1990 saw Clive Taylor stand down after

10 years as Editor, being replaced by Mike Williams for *Premier News* and Tony Gillam for *Premier Lines*. This was the first year of the *Crewe Luncheon*, an annual event which has grown into something of a Society institution. The Luncheons have all been ably organised by Ken Wood. In October 1990 a visit was arranged to the National Railway Museum where members were given 'behind the scenes' tours of closed areas of the museum to view stored artefacts and archive items, the party being shown around by Dr John Coiley, the Curator.

THE SOCIETY FROM 1991

The 1990s saw some additional events. In June 1992 David Patrick organised a visit to the signal boxes at Shrewbury attended by 30 members. Several new faces were noted, indicating the advantages of arranging a variety of activities to cater for different members' interests. In March 1995 Clive and Sue Taylor led a party of members on a tour of places of interest in Crewe. The following April John Shelley led a minibus tour of interesting sites in the Manchester area culminating in a tour of the museum at Liverpool Road.

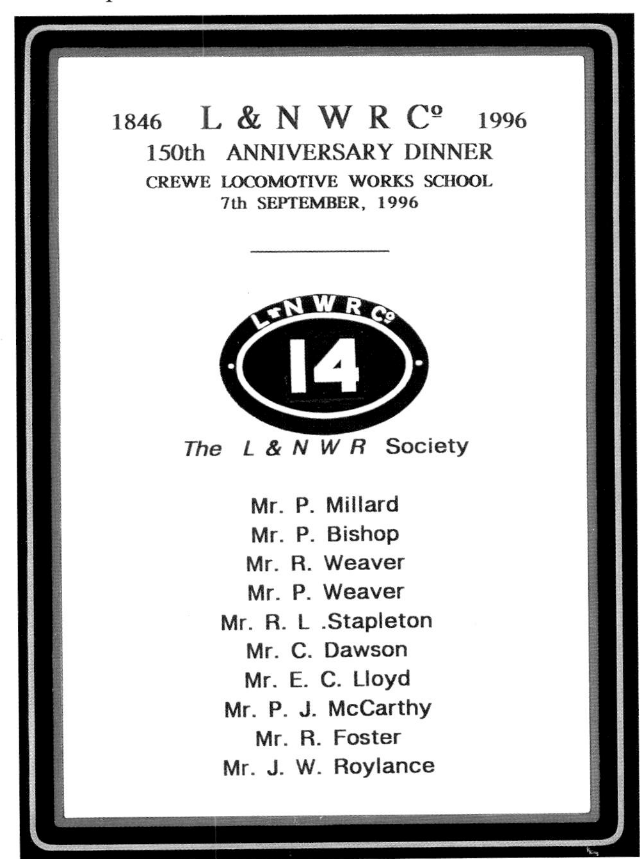
1846 L & N W R Cº 1996
150th ANNIVERSARY DINNER
CREWE LOCOMOTIVE WORKS SCHOOL
7th SEPTEMBER, 1996

The L & N W R Society

Mr. P. Millard
Mr. P. Bishop
Mr. R. Weaver
Mr. P. Weaver
Mr. R. L .Stapleton
Mr. C. Dawson
Mr. E. C. Lloyd
Mr. P. J. McCarthy
Mr. R. Foster
Mr. J. W. Roylance

Menu and table list for one of the Society tables at the 150th Anniversary Dinner in Crewe Works in 1996.

The year 1996 brought the 150th Anniversary of the formation of the LNWR. Ken Wood, irrepressible as ever, organised a special *Crewe Luncheon* in July, while ABB/Adtranz, the owners of Crewe Works, hosted a celebratory evening Dinner and Reception in the Works on 7th September, where the Society was represented by 30 members out of the 170 participants. Ken Wood contributed displays and also found time to organise a huge display and Society stand at the Crewe Works Open Day on 17th August (wow!). There were also contributions to the various events by a large number of Society members.

In September 1997 there were visits to the East Lancashire Railway and to the Diggle, Halebarns and Westport 0-gauge railway. The latter is located in John Penn's garden, and was originally constructed by Ken Longbottom. This visit was repeated in 1998. Over the late 1990s Chris Northedge organised a Society display of models and photographs at the Crewe Heritage Centre, with a different theme each year. Examples included *Carrying Goods* and *Passenger Traffic*.

In 2003 a membership survey was carried out and the percentages interested in each 'interest area' were as follows:

Area of Interest	%
Locomotives	76
Carriages	55
Photographs	54
Stations	51
Wagons	48
Books	44
Routes	38
Signalling	38
Civil Engineering	27
Timetables	25
Postcards	21
Artefacts	19
Performance	19
Letters	15

There were two very significant developments in the 2000s. The first was the granting of Charitable Status to the Society in 2005. A number of members spent a lot of time preparing the application and carrying it through, Dave Pennington and Christopher Hill being particularly heavily involved. The 'success first time' is a huge credit to them.

After much abortive work, we at last found a home for the Society's library and archive at member Richard Powell's business premises in Kenilworth. The rental agreement commenced on 1st December 2008, and the rooms were fitted out and the archives and library material moved in over the next few months. A significant proportion of the set-up costs were covered by a generous bequest from founder member Jeremy Flegg. The new 'Jeremy Flegg Study Centre' was officially opened by Roger Bell, Society President, on 4th April 2009. The vast majority of the work needed to set up the Centre, prepare all the documentation and arrange the moves, was undertaken by our Librarian and Archivist, Dave Pennington.

THE SOCIETY AS A CHARITY

The Society became a Registered Charity in 2005. This provides significant benefits in demonstrating the status of the Society and that there are protective arrangements in place for the security of the archive and library material. This status is very valuable when dealing with outside bodies, and provides confidence that donated material will be cared for and has a secure future. Similarly it gives confidence that cash donations will be used to further the Society's objectives. A major benefit is the ability to reclaim income tax on subscriptions from members paying tax. This is currently worth around £3500 per year, which allows the Society to do much more in delivering public benefits. Obtaining Charitable Status might be regarded as the Society's coming of age.

Obtaining Charitable Status
By Dave Pennington

Charitable Status was first investigated as early as 1980 although not pursued further. During 2004 the Committee discussed the advantages and disadvantages and agreed that it was a major benefit. An application to become an educational charity was put together, comprising the application forms and evidence supporting our claims of provision of 'public good'. A draft Constitution was written which re-cast the existing rules into the Charity Commission standard model. All this resulted in a large A4 ring binder full of material. Advice from the L&YR Society, who had previously applied successfully and from Philip Millard who was involved in the HMRS application was very helpful in getting our application right.

The application was submitted in November 2004. After answering some simple questions and simplifying the objects to identify more clearly the 'public good', we received outline approval in January 2005. The revised Constitution was approved at the 2005 AGM and final confirmation of our Charitable Status was received in June 2005.

We had to adopt the official name for the Society as 'LNWR Society' to avoid confusion with the existing "London & North Western Society" charity based at Chasewater, although we are able to use the fully expanded title on letter-heads etc.

SOCIETY ACTIVITIES

Meetings

A pattern of two meetings a year was quickly established, the AGM in the spring, initially in February but gradually drifting to May, and another in October/November. Usually there was a speaker or a tour or visit to things of LNWR interest in the local area. Members brought photographs, artefacts and models for display. Initially meetings were at Crewe Library, but after some complaints that 'Crewe was not very accessible'(!) the meetings were moved to Birmingham in 1979.

Our initial venue in Birmingham was the British Rail Staff Association Club in St. Vincent Street, which had a nice big hall where there was plenty of room for the meeting as well as for displays and moving about. The place had been built for the railwaymen of Monument Lane loco shed, carriage shed and goods depot, but by the time we arrived all had gone. Inevitably it closed in 1983. Curiously, some twenty years later the site became a venue again – the National Indoor Arena!

After a session at the Birmingham & Midland Institute, meetings moved in 1984 to another BR staff association club, in Inkerman Street, conveniently located a couple of minutes walk from Vauxhall (now Duddeston) station in Birmingham, which had an even larger hall. Some very interesting exhibitions were put on in the space alongside the meetings.

In 1990 it was decided that the Annual General Meetings ought to move around to attract members from different parts of the country. Chester was the venue for the 1990 AGM, followed by three years at Bletchley, after which the AGM has been in a different location each year. While speakers were initially the usual form of after-AGM entertainment, from the late 1990s AGMs have normally been followed by a local tour or visit.

AGM

10.30 am, April 19th 1980,
at the

BRITISH RAIL STAFF ASSOC. CLUB

St. Vincents Street, Birmingham.

Bar & Light Refreshments will be available during the lunch break.

The Society is represented at a number of modelling and model engineering exhibitions. This provides an opportunity to promote the Society, provide information on the LNWR, and attract new members. Where possible, we sell Society publications to help Society funds. For the members who volunteer to man the stands, it provides an excellent opportunity to meet new people and old friends and to talk about their favourite railway! We are always looking for new volunteers to help with this pleasurable way of publicising the Society. The photo shows the stand at the 2011 Telford exhibition with Francis Pearce, Roger Stapleton, Simon Fountain and Brian Hayes in attendance. The 0 gauge locos and carriages on the stand were built by Francis, and the 'Jubilee' 4-4-0 by Roger. (Simon Fountain)

LNWR SOCIETY ANNUAL GENERAL MEETINGS

YEAR	LOCATION	SPEAKER/EVENT
1973	Crewe Library	Start-Up AGM
1974	Crewe Library	
1975	Crewe Library	TW Bourne, Non-Passenger Coaching Stock
1976	Crewe Library	
1977	Crewe Library	C Sweeting, Watford & its Locos
1978	Crewe Library	
1979	Birmingham BRSA St. Vincent St	N Williamson, Compounding & Webb
1980	Ditto	PA Millard, Modelling LNWR Carriages
1981	Ditto	D Rowland, LNWR Wagons
1982	Ditto	Exhibition
1983	Birmingham Midland Institute	
1984	Birmingham BRSA Inkerman St	P Ellis, LNWR goods rolling stock
1985	Ditto	P Davis, Webb Compounds (substitute for K Cantlie)
1986	Ditto	H Jack, LNWR myth and history
1987	Ditto	JFB Stevens, 7mm layout of W S Norris
1988	Ditto	Coach tour of LNWR sites
1989	Birmingham Railway Museum, Tyseley	Tour of museum
1990	Chester St. Mary's Centre	J Gahan, LNWR in Liverpool area
1991	Bletchley Leisure Centre	P Lee, LNWR in Warwickshire & Leicestershire
1992	Ditto	P Davis, Crewe first essay in standardisation
1993	Ditto	Dr D Drummond, Crewe Works 1843-1914
1994	Crewe Victoria Centre	P Bishop, LNWR Electric trains
1995	York National Railway Museum	Super D restoration & tour
1996	Oxford Community Centre	N Lee & CS Taylor, LNWR photographs show
1997	Ditto	R Foster, LNWR Signalling
1998	Manchester Museum of Science & T.	Tour of museum
1999	Birmingham Railway Museum	Videos & tour of museum
2000	Milton Keynes Museum	Tour of museum & Wolverton
2001	Rainhill Library	Tour of Earlestown & area
2002	Buckinghamshire Railway Centre	Tour of exhibits
2003	Bury Old White Lion Hotel	Visit to East Lancs. Railway
2004	Keighley Innkeepers Lodge	Visit to Keighley & Worth Valley Railway
2005	Dudley Black Country Museum	Tour of museum
2006	Butterley Midland Railway Centre	Tour of West Shed and site
2007	Birmingham Thinktank Museum	D Pennington
2008	York Railway Institute	Visit to National Railway Museum
2009	Northampton Brampton Hall Pub	Visit to Northampton & Lamport Railway
2010	Chester Premier Queen Hotel	Coach tour of LNWR sites
2011	Quainton Memorial Hall	Visit to Buckinghamshire Railway Centre
2012	London Camden Pirate Castle	Tour of Camden Railway Heritage Trail
2013	Loughborough Gt. Central Rly.	Train trip hauled by Coal Tank

Society Open Day Meetings

The Society autumn meetings had changed from talks to an exhibition format very early on. The aims were to display things of LNWR interest, particularly models and photographs, but also artefacts, plans and documents, in a venue where there was room for members and visitors to come along, meet each other and talk about their favourite railway. They were designated 'Society Open Days'. Because they relied on members and others volunteering to bring material, models and model railway layouts, content could be a little varied and unpredictable, and no admission charges were made (donations encouraged!). Up until 1990 these were held in Birmingham at St. Vincent Street and Inkerman Street.

The early Open Days were organised by John Shelley, David Clarke, and Colin Reed among others. They all put a great deal of work and effort into persuading people to bring along things of interest. Each usually managed to secure at least one model railway layout (sometimes several!), stands by one or more traders, and displays of models (including some pretty large ones), a test track, photographs, plans etc, not to mention space for people to chat, eat and drink!

The 1984 Open Day featured three model railway layouts (Uppingham, Penlan (both EM) and Wolverley (7mm)), four trade stands, displays of models, signalling and paintings, sales stands for Society publications and copies of archive items. There was also a film show. London Road was the layout at the 1987 event, when 67 people signed the visitor's book. The signed-in attendance at the 1989 event was 150 when London Road was again on display, along with a Gauge 1 4-6-2 Prince tank, a 3½ inch gauge live steam 2-2-2-0 *Jeanie Deans,* together with a number of 0 gauge models and several trade stands.

The British Rail Staff Association club premises at Inkerman Street, which had been so ideal for us in terms of size, facilities, location and price, closed in the summer of 1992, and the autumn 1992 Open Day moved to a sports and social club in Rugby. There were three layouts, two trade stands, sales stands and exhibits. The 1993 event was similar with two layouts, different models, including some by Denis Nix and Geoff Williams, and a bookseller.

After a break in 1995, Richard Powell took on the task of organising the open days, initially in Birmingham and moving to Chilvers Coton Heritage Centre in Nuneaton from 1997. In October 1999 the venue moved again, to a school in Barrow-on-Soar, where the Society arranged a test track, exhibits and sales stands. The 2000 event had to be cancelled at short notice 'due to a national fuel crisis', and was rearranged for February 2001. Following discussions at the AGM the February date was retained 'to give a better spread of events through the year'. In 2003 the date moved to April so that the event could form part of the annual Gauge 0 exhibition at Barrow-on-Soar. The venue later moved to a school at Shepshed, again 'piggybacking' with the Gauge 0 exhibition. The last of these events took place in 2011.

At Homes

A new development in 1977 was the operation of two 'at homes' or open days at members' homes, where members were welcome to come along, chat about their favourite railway and bring models, drawings, and other items for discussion. These first two meetings were at the homes of Richard Foster and David Clarke. Following the success of these, great efforts were made to organise a programme of 'at homes' and in 1978 they were held at Richard Foster's in January and December, Jack Nelson's in February and Dudley Whitworth's in October. There were nine at homes in 1979 and generally between two and eight a year through to about 2000. Unfortunately after this they slowly petered out.

PREMIER NEWS, NEWSLETTERS AND JOURNALS

LONDON AND NORTH WESTERN RAILWAY SOCIETY

PREMIER LINES

NO. 31 February 1980

The new cover header for *Premier Lines* introduced in February 1980.

In February 1980 Sandy Croall took temporary charge of *Premier News.* He introduced a new publication *Premier Lines* as 'an attempt to bring together the various articles that normally 'float' around the newsletter'. Effectively *Premier Lines* took on the material that had previously been issued as separate papers and pamphlets, while *Premier News* continued

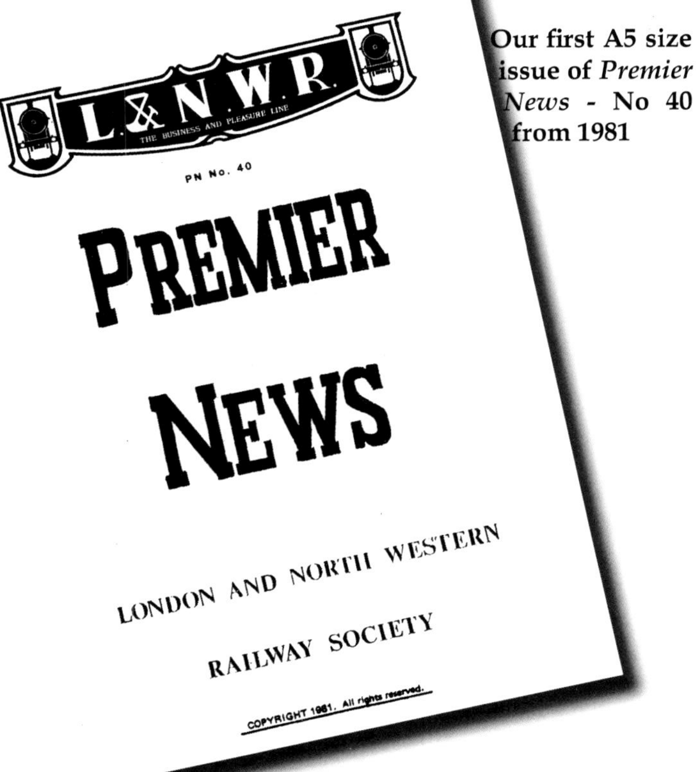

Our first A5 size issue of *Premier News* - No 40 from 1981

with a mix of Society and general news and snippets on the LNWR. Longer papers continued to be issued separately. Clive Taylor took on the Editor's role from September 1980.

With *Premier News 39* (Summer 1981) the method of printing was changed to photocopying. This was but the prelude to a much more fundamental change. From *PN40* the format changed to A5 folded, effectively a magazine at last. There was a new cover design, but content continued to be typewritten and printing was by photocopying. The new A5 *PN* was 12 pages, expanding to 16 pages in March 1983.

Over the 1980 to 1984 period the roles of *Premier News* and *Premier Lines* changed. *Premier Lines* only appeared occasionally and the articles it had contained migrated to *Premier News. Premier Lines* became regular again from 1984, but it now contained Society and other news, questions and book reviews, while *PN* contained articles and LNWR material. Each *Premier Lines* was titled, 'Addendum to Premier News (or Portfolio) No XX', and between 1980 and 1990 were generally undated, making them a little difficult to follow!

To mark the 50th issue of *PN*, a printed glossy cover was used, incorporating four photographs. This was the first time printed photographs had appeared in the *PN*. This was just the prelude to the big breakthrough which came with *PN* 52 in July 1984. While Clive Taylor continued as Editor, the tasks of production and printing for *PN* were separated and Barry Lane, who was already responsible for the L&YR Society's excellent *Platform* magazine, took on these very important tasks.

With Barry's experienced hands in control of production, there was an immediate step-change in the appearance and quality of *PN*. Issue 52 appeared with better quality paper, a card cover with coloured title and photographs to illustrate the articles. Ten years of hard work had borne fruit, now at last we had a journal we could be proud of. The *PNs* slowly increased in size, from 12 to 20 pages in 1984, and to 24 pages in 1986. *PL* varied between two and eight pages.

By 1990 Clive Taylor had done a sterling ten years as Editor, and following his marriage in 1989 he stepped down. In view of the growing workload it was decided to split responsibilities for *Premier News* and *Premier Lines*. Fortunately two very capable people appeared at the right time to take up the reins, Mike Williams took on the job of Editor of *PN* and Tony Gillam became the *PL* (newsletter) Editor. Production was standardised on a regular schedule of March, June, September and December – still the case today. Behind the scenes, Barry Lane continued his excellent work on production and printing. Without the need to prioritise work on *PN*, Tony Gillam was able to revolutionise *PL*, which took on a new appearance and jumped in size to 12 pages. The first issues under their new editors were No. 79 of September 1990. Over the next three years

The special cover to mark the 50th issue of *Premier News*

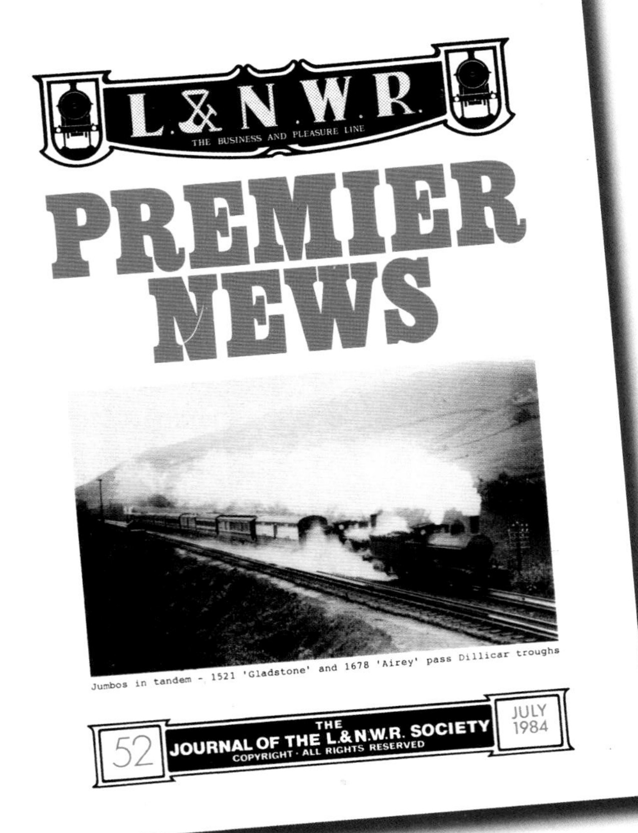

The new cover design for the first printed *Premier News* which included photographs. This cover layout continued through to No 91, the last *Premier News* in 1993.

Premier Lines

The newsletter of the London & North Western Railway Society

No.79 September 1990

SLIPPERY START FROM EUSTON ...
... AND WORRYING ABOUT CAMDEN BANK

You should have gathered by now that both Premier News and Premier Lines have new hands on the footplate. Mike Williams and I are beginning to wonder how Clive Taylor ever managed to drive and fire on his own. He's probably riding 'on the cushions' waiting for the sounds of our first slip! The Chief Guard G.R.Thomson Esq. is still fulminating about starting on time, while quietly arranging for an extra three bogies.

More seriously, I'll try to keep my own jottings under control and avoid a preponderance of purple prose mixed with musings of muddled metaphor. The change of editor does call for an explanation of proposed policies regarding publications. It is the firm intention to publish on time; four times a year in March, June, September and December. I'm aiming for an interesting read. Any society publication is only as good as the copy supplied and no editor wants to write it all himself (hint hint). See the back page for further details about where to send items.

IMPORTANT DATES

Sat. 22nd September 1990 "Living & Forgotten Railways at Crewe" led by H. Forster. Railway & Canal Historical Society outing, our members invited. Party (max.20 total) leaves Crewe Station Booking Hall 10.30am.

Sat. 6th October 1990 11am to 5pm. 'At Home' with Dave Pennington 28 Quebec Gardens, Blackwater, Camberley, Surrey GU17 9DE. Please phone 0276 31252 in advance to say you wish to attend. The Library and archives will be on show and refreshments will be provided. Please bring items or models of LNW interest to stimulate discussion.

Sat. 20th October 1990 Society visit to York NRM. Last chance now to send back the yellow booking form. Special things will be laid on for the visit, but ...... IT WILL ONLY HAPPEN IF THERE IS A GOOD RESPONSE!

Sat. 10th November 1990 Autumn meeting at BRSA Club, Inkerman Street, Birmingham. Doors open 11am. Various traders, 2 or 3 layouts, Society stands etc. Bring your models to display and discuss. I expect it will be the usual menu that you have come to know and love. Map on yellow sheet.

Sat. 24th November 1990 Society Lunch at the Crewe Arms Hotel with after lunch speaker. See yellow form from last mailing for full details.

Sat. 11th May 1991 AGM 1991. 11am, Bletchley Leisure Centre. More details and a map nearer the time.

1

The first *Premier Lines* to go out under Tony Gillam's Editorship, with typical editorial, and a tantalising advert for one of the Inkerman Street Events – happy memories!

Mike Williams developed *PN* further, with the number of pages in each issue increasing each year, reaching 44 in December 1992, while *PL* increased to 16 pages in 1991.

The increased income from the subscription rise in 1993 enabled Mike Williams and Barry Lane to put forward a proposal for an upgrade of *PN*. The idea was to increase the page size to A4 and use better quality paper and printing processes, with a change in title to *The L&NWR Society Journal*. The last issue of *PN* was No 91 of September 1993, and the first issue of the *Journal* appeared in December 1993 (*Journal* Volume 1 No 1). The resultant step change in quality and appearance of our magazine is a lasting tribute to the work put in by Mike and Barry. It gave us a journal which was (and is) one of the best in the field. Twelve months later, *Premier Lines* changed its name to *The Newsletter* (No 96, December 1994).

After a daunting 14 years as *Newsletter* Editor, Tony Gillam, stepped down. His last *Newsletter* was No 135 of September 2004. Christopher Hill stood in temporarily for the December 2004 issue, changing the format from A5 to A4 to match the *Journal*. Dave Pennington stepped in temporarily after Christopher's death, with Stephen Weston taking on the Editorship from September 2006.

Stephen Weston had to step down as *Newsletter* Editor at the end of 2012. Fortunately, a volunteer emerged to take on the role, in the form of Tony Gillam (where have we heard that name before?), perhaps the ultimate glutton for punishment! Tony, hopefully fully revitalised, produced his first 'new' *Newsletter* in March this year.

Returning to the *Journal*, after over 15 years as Editor, Mike Williams stood down on completion of Volume 4 and thus the March 2006 issue was his last. Barry Lane, who had undertaken the design and production of *PN* and the *Journal* for an incredible 21½ years (not to mention undertaking the distribution, jointly with his wife, Ann, for many of them!) also finished his work at the same time. Service indeed! The Society owes them all a great deal for the effort they have put in.

Journal Volume 5 No 1 (June 2006) saw a new team in the shape of John Stockton-Wood as Editor and Peter Chatham for design and production. Peter brought in electronic methods for his layout design and production work. Unfortunately, John had to step down at the beginning of 2009 for family reasons and his place was taken by Stephen Weston. Stephen, too, had to stand down, although fortunately he continued until a replacement could be found. Peter Chatham also decided to finish at the same time so that he would have a bit more time for his modelling and clocks. As well as undertaking the (unsung) *Journal* design and production work,

ISSN 1352-2833
THE L&NWR SOCIETY
JOURNAL
INCORPORATING 'PREMIER NEWS'
Volume 1 Number 1 December 1993

The great step forward in *Journal* quality - The first of the A4 size *Journals*

1994

AT HOMES

Thank you to those who have run an event in the recent past. We seek volunteers for more events, particularly in the North and Wales/West. Can you help? Contact Dave Pennington for assistance if you are unsure about how to arrange an "At Home". ☎ 0276 31252

IMPORTANT DATES

Sat. 11TH MARCH 1995, Peter Turville of Derby. 11am to 5pm. This is a very popular event and books up rapidly so you need to contact Peter early if you wish to attend. A buffet lunch is provided at a nominal charge with proceeds going to *The Picnic Saloon Trust*. Send an s.a.e for a map of the location. "The Firs", Nether Heage, Derby. DE5 2AT.

Sat. 18th March 1995, an open day at Robert Head's, Shifnal. Bill Broadbent is liasing over this, and he wishes to gauge members' interest. Last time, the level of attendance by members was poor, although everyone else had a marvellous time. If you are interested, please tell Bill a.s.a.p, at: Pembroke Cottage, Crockwell Street, Long Compton, Shipston-on-Stour, Warwickshire CV36 5JN. (Please send a s.s.a.e if a reply is needed)

Sat. 29TH APRIL 1995, Dave Pennington (Librarian) of Camberley. 11 am to 5pm. The Society library and archives will be available for browsing and archive copies will be on sale. The computer based bibliography can be used for searching out references. A demonstration of the HMRS PhotoCAT can also be provided. Send a s.s.a.e for a map. 28 Quebec Gardens, Blackwater, Camberley, Surrey. GU17 9DE.

Sat. 13TH MAY 1995. LNWR Society Annual General Meeting. The National Railway Museum, Leeman Road, York. Also Richard Gibbon talking about (and demonstrating?) progress with the Super 'D' and/or Dieter Hopkin on a tour of the library facilities (and how to use them). No charge for attendance, although voluntary donations will be encouraged by the Society. Full details in the next newsletter.

/continued ...

1

From December 1994 the name *Premier Lines* was dropped, and our newsletter became simply *The Newsletter* although the number series was continued.

Peter had taken on quite a bit of the work normally undertaken by the editor to help Stephen through his difficult times, not to mention production work on a couple of our publications.

After much searching, a new team came forward in the form of Chris Northedge as Editor and Peter Meyer for production, their first *Journal* being that for March 2013. This saw the innovation of the inclusion of colour photographs. Thus the Society is entering its 40th year with new blood at the helms of both the *Journal* and the *Newsletter!*

PUBLICATIONS

The problem of publication quality, and particularly the desire to publish photographs, exercised the minds of the Committee almost from the beginning. The first venture into publishing something of better quality and with photographs was made in 1977, with the publication of *The Friezland Accident of 1909*. It contained photographs for the first time, and was effectively a half-way house between the pamphlets and the portfolios which followed. Considering the printing method and paper the photograph reproduction was quite reasonable.

The pressure to find ways of publishing photographs and drawings in a better quality publication led to the publication of *Premier Portfolios* Numbers 1 and 2 in the first half of 1983. These were printed on art paper, and used a larger page size, allowing high quality reproduction of drawings and photographs. They were the brain-child of David Clarke, who compiled them and organised their printing. They contained a miscellany of items, which for quality reasons could not be used in *Premier News* at the time. With the improvements in *Premier News* in 1984, this miscellany format for special publications was no longer needed, and all further publications have been on single subjects, but David had set the path.

The series title *Premier Portfolio* was used for our new publications between 1983 and 2004, over which period a total of 16 titles were produced, several of which ran to second editions. *Portfolio No 3* on *LNWR Locomotive Nameplates* was the first single subject portfolio, being a revised version, now with illustrations, of a *Premier Pamphlet* of 1980.

After the appearance of *Portfolio No 16, LNWR Houses*, in 1984, the series title *Premier Portfolio* was dropped and all further publications have been titled as stand-alone productions. A particular landmark was reached in 2006, when the Society produced its first (and currently only!) hard-backed book *LNWR Non-Corridor Carriages*, by Philip Millard and Ian Tattersall. This ran to 136 pages packed with detailed information, photographs and drawings. The authors and Peter Chatham, who did the production work (remember he was also producing *Journals*), deserve a huge amount of credit for the superb book that resulted from all their hard work.

There can be no publications without authors, and we need to give thanks to our many authors who have given so much of their free time to researching and writing, for our benefit but for no financial reward to themselves. In addition, there can be no publications without someone to organise the production, and liaise with the printers. While the author at least gets his name on the cover, the production person's work behind the scenes can often go unrecorded. Among others our thanks are due to David Clarke, Clive Taylor, Barry Lane, Paul Rouet, Roy Thomson, Peter Chatham and David Moore, with apologies to anyone who has been omitted. Especial thanks are due to Ted Talbot, who has had responsibility in whole, or in part, for the majority of the publications that have been produced since around 2005. In addition, Ted's work has not been confined to getting the publication produced, he has actively sought out authors, nurtured them and helped with finding illustrations.

THE WEBB SITE

The Society originally set up an internet website around 2000. Chris Hill took on the webmaster role in 2002 having his new 'Webb' (for fairly obvious reasons!) site fully operational by early summer. He followed up by doing a huge amount of work developing the site and adding material prior to his untimely death in 2005.

Fortunately David Moore rose to the challenge and agreed to take on responsibility for the site. Subsequently David has spent a vast amount of time and effort in developing and expanding the site. It now contains a phenomenal amount of information and users have a lot to thank David for.

Internet Forum

This was set up in 2009 and is moderated and administered by David Moore. The material on the forum is publicly accessible, but only members can post material on it.

APPEALS

There have been two appeals for funds to support particular 'restoration' projects which have been operated through the Society – for an authentic chimney for the 'Super D' 0-8-0 locomotive at the National Railway Museum, and for authentic front and tail lamps for the Coal Tank. In addition, the Society hosted the dissemination of information on the restoration of the LNWR picnic saloon by the Picnic Saloon Trust.

The restoration of the LNWR Super D 0-8-0 had been long-promised practically ever since it was withdrawn in 1959. After many false starts, the National Railway Museum took on the restoration to working order, but indicated that they would do this to BR external condition, a significant proportion of the funding coming from Pete Waterman. The Society launched an appeal to raise funds to allow a new, LNWR-style, chimney to be fitted to the locomotive. As with most such appeals it took some time to accumulate the necessary money. Eventually, on 12th March 1993 our chairman, Paul Rouet and member John Crawley travelled to York to officially hand over the cheque to Andrew Dow, Curator of the Museum.

In 1999 the Coal Tank 1054 was undergoing its ten year major overhaul on the Keighley & Worth Valley Railway. To help restore it to as near its Pre-Gouping appearance as possible, the Society launched an appeal in December 1999 for funds to have a set of replica LNWR locomotive headlamps made. It was estimated that these would cost around £600.

In the event things took a lot longer than expected. It was a long time before the final restoration of the locomotive was completed, while the Society had considerable difficulties finding someone to make the lamps. Eventually the lamps were made by Alf Peach and completed at the end of 2011, the final cost being £1,600, a slight increase on the original estimate! Five lamps were made, one being retained by Alf Peach. There was a 'launch party' for the Coal Tank on the Keighley & Worth Valley Railway on 8th February 2012, when Peter Stanton presented the four lamps to the Bahamas Locomotive Society on behalf of the Society (see the cover of *Journal* Vol 7 No 1 June 2012 for a photograph of the engine with one of the lamps in place).

The model of Super D 49395 which was commissioned by the LNWR Society and presented to Pete Waterman on 22nd April 2006 in recognition of the input of time, hard work and money, he put in to ensure the restoration to working order of the full-size locomotive. As can be seen, the builder, Geoff Holt, did the Society and Pete proud – the work is superb. It is a lasting tribute to Geoff too. Just study the detail!

(Tony Wright, courtesy British Railway Modelling)

The Super D Award and Model, by Richard Foster

As mentioned in the 'Appeals' section above, Pete Waterman provided much of the funding for the restoration to working order of 'Super D' 0-8-0 49395. The Society felt that his generosity deserved some recognition. We consulted Geoff Holt, one of our members and who had made a number of models for Pete's model layout. He suggested that a model of the 'Super D' itself would be very appropriate. The Society therefore commissioned Geoff to make the 7mm model. This was completed early in 2006, and opportunity was taken at the Gauge 0 Exhibition and Society Open Day at Shepshed on 22nd April to present the model to Pete Waterman in recognition of his contribution to the 'Super D' restoration. Effectively this award could be considered to be the fore-runner of our Premier Line Awards.

Geoff Holt was an accomplished model-maker of long standing and, as can be seen from the photographs, he did a superb job on 49395. A real gentleman, and superbly knowledgeable and accomplished, I have known Geoff for many years through our mutual membership of the LMS Society. After he retired, as well as his own model-making, he made models professionally to order, mainly of LNWR and LMS types. A favourite approach, when accepting a commission, was to make two models at the same time, one for the client and one for himself. Unfortunately he died in April this year, leaving a big gap in the field of quality model making.

A close-up detail of th interior of the cab of th model of 49395. Geoff Ho certainly did detail! No the colours of the inside c the cab side sheets and roo
(Tony Wrigh courtesy Britis Railway Modellin

LNWRS OFFICERS

Chairmen

Eric Rayner	1973 - 1975
Richard Foster	1975 - 1988
Roy Thomson	1988 - 1992
Paul Rouet	1992 - 2004
Peter Stanton	2004 - 2013
Brian Hayes	2013 -

Secretaries

Robert Ormiston-Chant	1973 - 1975
Graham Thomas	1975 - 1978
Sandy Croall	1978 - 1980
David Clarke	1980 - 1981
Geoff Williams	1982 - 1988
Andy Lowe	1988 - 2003
Simon Fountain	2003 -

Treasurers

Dudley Whitworth	1973 - 1981
Roy Thomson	1981 - 1986
Denis Nix	1987 - 2000
Bob Williams	2000 - 2010
Martin O'Keeffe	2010 -

Editors

Premier News, Premier Pamphlets etc

Robert Ormiston-Chant	1973 - 1975
David Clarke	1975 - 1980
Clive Taylor	1980 - 1990
Mike Williams	1990 - 1993

The Journal

Mike Williams	1993 - 2006
John Stockton-Wood	2006 - 2009
Stephen Weston	2009 - 2012
Christopher Northedge	2013 -

Premier Lines

David Clarke	1975 - 1980
Clive Taylor	1980 - 1990
Tony Gillam	1990 - 1994

Newsletter

Tony Gillam	1994 - 2004
Christopher Hill	2004 - 2005
Dave Pennington	2005 - 2006
Stephen Weston	2006 - 2012
Tony Gillam	2013 –

Membership Secretary

Christopher Hill	2002 - 2005
Peter Stanton (temporary)	2005 - 2006
Brian Harris	2006 - 2011
Alan Shepherd	2011 -

Librarian & Archivist

Mike Warren	1980 - 1982
Dave Pennington	1982 -

Photographic Officer

Mike Bland	1975 - 1988
Norman Lee	1988 -

Drawings Officer

Richard Foster	1975 - 1986
Roy Thomson	1986 - 1991
Paul Rouet	1991 - 2009
Ray Berry	2011 - 2012
Tony Simmonds	2012 -

Webmaster

Christopher Hill	2002 - 2005
David Moore	2005 -

Modelling Officer

David Clarke	1974 - 1980
John Dale	1991 - 1997
Ray Stacey	1998 - 2004
Peter Stanton	2005 - 2013
Philip Millard	2013 -

Exhibitions, Special Events & Promotions Officers

Events and open meetings arranged by a number of individual members over the years.

Simon Fountain	2004 - 2012
Ken Wood	1990 -
Jol Wilkinson	2006 - 2013
Peter Stanton	2013 -

Journal & Newsletter Production & Distribution

Barry Lane	1984 - 2006
Peter Chatham	2006 - 2012
Peter Meyer	2013 -
Graham Hardy	1987 - 2000
Barry & Ann Lane	2001 - 2006
David Deakin	2006 - 2011
Tony Waterfield	2011 -

Sales Officers (New and Second-Hand)

John Shelley	1985 - 1988
Eddy Bray	1988 - 1994
MaryAnn Lowe	1995 - 2006
Tom Sherratt	2007 - 2010
Martin O'Shea	1997 -

Press Digest Coordinator

Neil Fraser	1998 - 2001
Chris James	2001 -

Auditors and Examiners

Geoff Platt & Philip Millard to 1980

Philip Millard	1980 - 1996
Bob Williams	1997 - 2000
Denis Nix	2000 - 2005
Philip Millard	2006 - 2008
Roy Thomson	2008 - 2009
Philip Millard	2010 -

LNWRS PRESIDENTS AND VICE-PRESIDENTS

Presidents

Eric Rayner	1975 - 1978
Jack Nelson	1978 - 1979
Bill Allen	1979 - 1980
Patrick Fisher	1980 - 1981
Dudley Whitworth	1981 - 1982
Ted Talbot	1982 - 1988
Richard Foster	1988 - 1993
Geoff Williams	1993 - 1999
Neil Fraser	2000 - 2002
Rodney Weaver	2002 - 2003
Harry Jack	2003 - 2006
Roger Bell	2006 - 2009
Ted Talbot	2009 - 2012
Roger Stapleton	2012 - 2013
Peter Skellon	2013 -

Vice-Presidents (year of election given)

Dudley Whitworth	1983
David Clarke	1983
Geoff Williams	1989
Ted Talbot	1989
Roy Thomson	1992
Richard Foster	1993
Clive Taylor	1993
Denis Nix	2000
Andy Lowe	2003
Barry Lane	2006
Harry Jack	2007
Mike Williams	2007
Paul Rouet	2008
Peter Chatham	2013
Martin O'Shea	2013

SPECIAL MEMBERS

This section looks at a small selection of past members, who are no longer with us, but who had interesting histories, contributed significantly to our knowledge and understanding of the LNWR or to the development of the Society, or a combination of them. Due to limitations of space it has only been possible to include a small selection of these people here. The personal profiles are presented in alphabetical order.

Bill Allen (right) with his guest, Terry Meredith, at the Crewe Lunch in 1995. (Tony Gillam)

Allen, William G – 'Bill'
Modeller, LNWR Society member, Society President 1979-80. By David Patrick

William (Bill) Allen was a family friend, being a colleague of my father's in the design office at Rolls-Royce from the late 1940s. He was born in 1912 and my early memories of him are of someone who would ring my father with instructions to meet him at Crewe station, usually well past my bedtime, where we would see something rather special. Sure enough we did, the Royal Train would pass through or sometimes stop to change engines. There would be standby 'Duchesses' in a state of cleanliness that was rarely seen in those days, glistening in the dimly-lit station. He would regale us with details of the various saloons which, at this period, were mainly of LNWR origin. How he obtained the actual time the 'Royal' was due was a mystery, until I found out that the source was from none other than the Chief Passenger Inspector of the Line Manager's office at Crewe and who was a near neighbour of his and who travelled on the 'Royals' to ensure their trouble-free progress.

On occasions, before his marriage to Barbara, he was in 'digs' and I would be invited to visit him, where he showed me many of his models, photographs and railway magazines and recounted his many memories of his railway experiences. He was probably responsible for my conversion from a mere 'train spotter' to becoming more seriously interested in railway history and operations.

Bill was an excellent scratch-build modeller, and his enthusiasm for the Midland Railway can be seen in the many models he produced for the Midland Railway exhibits in Derby museum. He was also interested in, and created models of, the steam fairground era and the railway vehicles that conveyed them around the country. He was known, even in advancing years, to be seen crawling and measuring beneath such vehicles that he had spotted before their final disintegration, with a view to modelling them.

Bill came from an LNWR family. His grandfather had been attached to the head office at Euston as a travelling inspector and trouble-shooter, finishing his career as Station Master at Rugby in the 1890s. His father also served the LNWR and became Station Master at Rhyl. It follows, therefore, that railways were in Bill's blood, but his father, having great foresight, saw that, by the 1930s, the railway industry was in decline. Bill therefore entered the motor-car industry in 1930, serving his premium apprenticeship at Arthur Mulliner's, the Northampton coachbuilder, moving in 1935 to Rolls-Royce at Derby, in their chassis design department. Rolls-Royce at that time was not building complete cars, merely the engine and chassis; you bought the body separately from the coachbuilder of your choice. In 1945 the car division relocated to the Crewe factory in Pym's Lane, which had been manufacturing Merlin engines during the war. Bill found himself in the body-styling section where he took a leading roll in all the well-known post-war models. During John Blatchely's (the head of design) illness Bill, as deputy, was responsible for the design of the 'Corniche' model. One of his lesser known achievements was a 'private commission' to draw up the body-design for the English Electric turbine locomotive GT3, probably one of the more attractive looking of the experimental locomotives of the period.

During one of my visits to his home, he related one event which happened on his daily journey to school from Northampton to Towcester. This involved a change of trains at Blisworth and on one occasion, whilst waiting for his connection, he heard a typical high-pitched LNWR whistle, and looking down the line, saw a locomotive with a very tall Webb chimney travelling very fast, but this being in the days of 'Georges', 'Precursors' and 'Claughtons', thought it unusual. In fact it was two Webb tank engines travelling light at high speed, possibly destined for Crewe Works for either overhaul or withdrawal. They ran through Blisworth in true LNWR fashion, whistles screaming, a reminder and vision of an earlier epoch, the drivers being intent on seeing what they could get out of the two antiques. This memory obviously impressed him, as he told me the tale more than once.

Bill was truly the railwayman he never was, being interested in all railways. I remember our family, together with Bill and Barbara, visiting the Talyllyn Railway in its early preservation days and his utter delight in its charm and idiosyncrasies. He also thoroughly enjoyed the meetings we held in Birmingham, and even when not in the best of health, he insisted on attending. His special interests in LNWR matters were of the workings of the Royal Train and its vehicles, and the TPO vehicles and workings. He was a great friend of Jim Richards, in fact staying at his home on numerous occasions. One can only imagine the conversations of two such knowledgeable experts; I doubt we shall see their like again.

Bill Allen was a true gentleman in the fullest meaning and without prejudice, seeing without fear or favour, the strengths and weaknesses of all the railway systems, and enjoying others' opinions and interests. He was extremely proud to be asked to be the Society's President, a truly worthy recipient.

Cantlie, Lt. Colonel, Kenneth, R.E., C Eng., F.I.Mech.E., F.P.W.I.
LNWR Crewe Apprentice, Distinguished Locomotive Engineer, LNWR Society Member.
By Richard Foster

Kenneth Cantlie's father, Sir James Cantlie was a surgeon and tropical diseases specialist, practising in Harley Street for many years. The family originated in Banffshire, Scotland. James married Mabel Barclay Brown in 1884. Kenneth, their fourth son, was born on 15th June 1899. He was christened at Cottered, Hertfordshire, where the family had a country home and was educated at Gordon's Academy, Aberdeen. At least one brother entered the medical profession, while Colin Cantlie joined the Royal Navy and rose to the rank of Lieut. Commander.

Kenneth developed a fascination for all things LNWR, especially locomotives, probably encouraged by C J Bowen Cooke who was a family friend, and went to Crewe as a Premium Apprentice between 1915 and 1919. He was involved with the building of the 'Claughton' Class engine *Patriot* and was a staunch 'Crewe Man' throughout his life. On his starting day Bowen Cooke told him 'Before you learn the job, learn the men and they will teach you the job'. He never forgot this advice. As well as time in the works and drawing office, he managed to spend a significant amount of time on the footplate of locomotives on ordinary and special services, learning about the strengths and weaknesses of locomotive designs and driving and firing techniques.

After his apprenticeship, he was appointed Assistant Locomotive Superintendent of the Entre Rios Railway, Argentina. Aged just 21, he sailed from Liverpool to Buenos Aires in October 1920. In 1924 he moved to India as Assistant Mechanical Engineer of the metre-gauge Jodhpur State Railway. There he designed new main line coaches, including some luxury vehicles for the Maharajah's special train, some of which were later used on Indian Railway's luxury metre-gauge tourist train.

The family had long associations with China. One of Sir James' medical students was Sun Yat Sen who became the first President of China. In 1896 Sir James' intervention through the Home Office saved the life of Dr Sun Yat Sen, who had been kidnapped by the Imperial Government's Agents in London. As a result the family was highly regarded in China, and when Sun Yat Sen, who had died in 1925, was reburied in a grand mausoleum in 1929, Kenneth represented the family at the ceremony. There he was invited to become technical advisor to the Chinese National Railway. He took up the post in 1930, after a study tour of USA railways.

In China he played a major part in the design of new locomotives and rolling stock, and the construction of new lines. He was responsible for the design of the KF Class 4-8-4s of which twenty-four were built at Vulcan Foundry, Newton-le-Willows in 1934-5.Cantlie used his studies of André Chapelon's work to ensure steam flow was efficient and he described these engines as the 'last true Crewe design'. They proved very successful and remained in service until 1974. He arranged for one of the class to be returned to Britain as a gift from the people of China. The hand-over ceremony took place in 1980, and the locomotive is currently on show in the Great Hall at the National Railway Museum.

He returned from China in 1937 for an eye operation, afterwards becoming Deputy Managing Director of Associated Locomotive Equipment Ltd., where he was involved in the application of Caprotti and Lentz poppet valve gears. He joined the Royal Engineers in 1939 and was in charge of military railways in the invasion area in 1940. At the end of the war he joined the Control Commission for Germany and was responsible for all heavy engineering firms in the Ruhr.

In 1948 he became Overseas Advisory Engineer to the Locomotive Manufacturers' Association, advising overseas railways and looking for potential export markets. He found potential for small orders, but the Association thought they had enough big orders and largely ignored his advice. He spent the summer of 1951 in America, doing things in style, travelling out on the Cunard White Star liner *Queen Elizabeth* (the original one!) and returning on *Queen Mary*. He returned to India after independence, where he played a large part in the design of a new locomotive works at Chitteranjan.

He was invited back to China in 1956 as guest of Premier Zhou Enlai to commemorate the 90th anniversary of Sun Yat Sen's birth. He was an enthusiast through and through and a long-standing member of the SLS, joining in 1949. In the early days of the LNWRS he gave a talk at one of the Society's meetings on his experiences as an Apprentice at

Crewe, during which his enquiring and razor-sharp mind shone out. I remember him saying that one of his early jobs was to run the bolt-cutting machine. Quickly becoming bored with this, he discovered how to run two machines at the same time, and then tried to add interest by 'racing' them against each other! If only we had recorded and written down all he said!

He continued as a Consulting Engineer on Locomotives and was active until shortly before his death. He died on 11th February 1986 at the age of 86.

(With thanks to Colin Garrett, George Carpenter, Roy Thomson and the SLS.)

Roy Thomson provided the following personal memories:

I met Cantlie on a number of occasions and served with him on the annual 'Crewe Dinner' Committee. It was I who persuaded him to come to Crewe and give us a talk about his days as a Premium Apprentice.

He only had sight in one eye and this resulted in him not being in the army in WW1. During the war he told me he used to travel home to London for weekends and served as a volunteer ambulance driver. Whilst apprenticed to C J Bowen Cooke he seems to have acted as the Chief Engineer's aide-de-camp and chauffeur and I believe this involved him in driving Bowen Cooke to and from the Chief's weekend retreat at Beeston Castle (I think).

We talked about the weaker points of the *Claughtons*, particularly of them being 'under-boilered'. He had two theories about this. One was that the Board would not agree to the expense of providing a set of new Press Tools for a new design of loco. Alternatively, there may have been opposition from the Chief Civil Engineer to increased axle loading and what effect this would have had on the permanent way. I think Cantlie made himself very unpopular with the Civil Engineer by insisting he was quite wrong about the axle loads as the danger came from 'hammer blow' not dead weight and with four cylinders driving on the same axle on the *Claughton* 'hammer blow' was kept to a minimum.

Kenneth said that in LMS days he visited Camden Shed and his attention was drawn to a *Cauliflower*. There was a problem, either a cracked frame or hot boxes or both. He looked between the frames and saw that the centre frame had been removed. Apparently this had been done as an LMS economy measure, one less axle box to maintain! He said it was hard to believe that FWW would have spent money in providing that extra bearing if it wasn't really required.

He told me that on one occasion he had been on the footplate during a special run of Trevithic 2-2-2 *Cornwall* (built way back in 1847), taking the Chief Mechanical Engineer's saloon back to Watford, in which a speed approaching 100 mph was reached on the Trent Valley section. He seemed to be very fond of this story.

A Cantlie Letter

The following lovely letter appeared in the SLS Journal in 1951 and sums up his no-nonsense and direct approach. His direct hands-on experience of real work with LNWR locomotives shines through. Pure Cantlie!

To the Editor,

THE L. & N.W.R. "EXPERIMENT" CLASS

I have read the letter of Mr. Neville in your May 1950 issue, and the reply of Mr. Arnott in your July 1950 issue with interest.

Extract from the Crewe Works Staff Register recording Kenneth Cantlie's transfer from Mr Roscoe's to Mr Price's Department in June 1917. Note the 'No Pay' comment in the pay rate column, reflecting his 'Premium Apprentice' status.

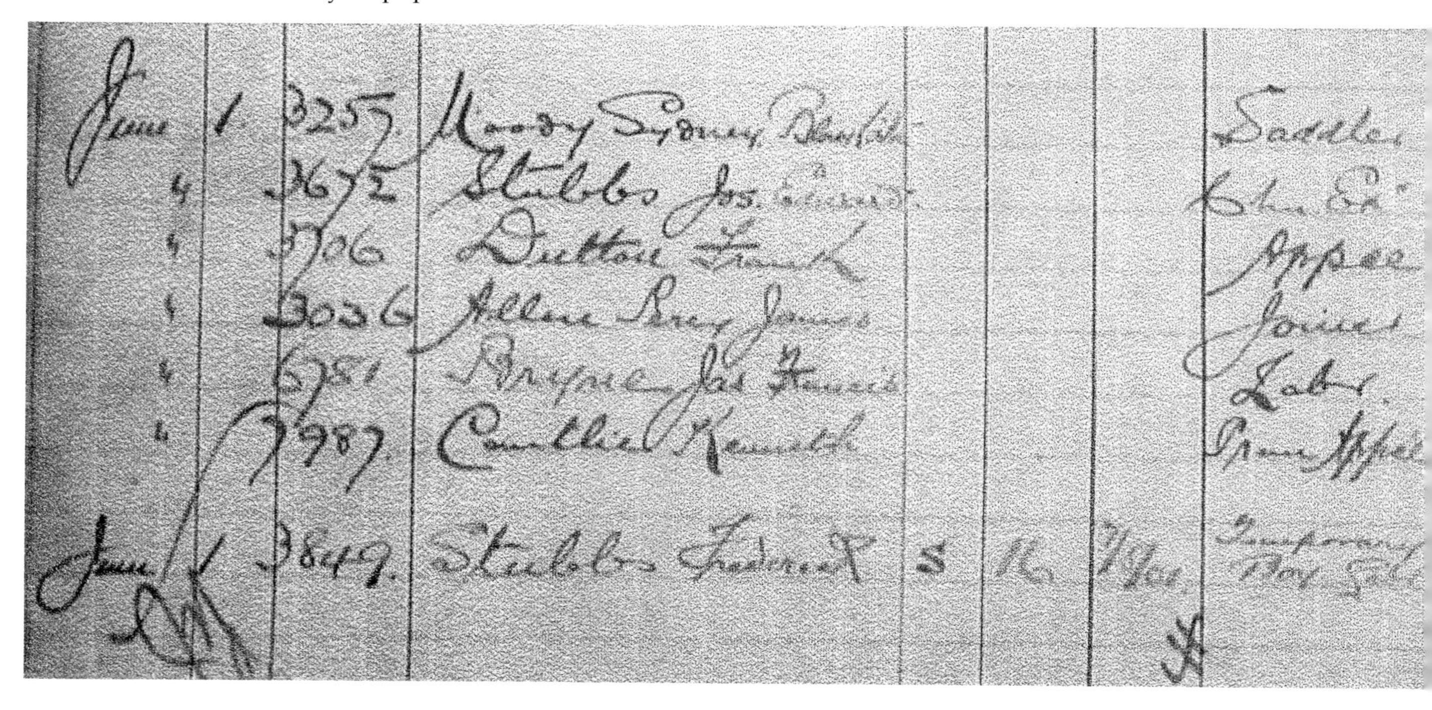

June	1	3257	Moody Sydney [illegible]				Saddler
	4	3672	Stubbs Jos. [illegible]				[illegible]
	4	3706	Dutton Frank				Apprce
	4	3036	Allen Percy James				Joiner
	4	6781	[illegible] Jas Francis				Labr
	4	3987	Cantlie Kenneth				Prem Apprce
June	1	3849	Stubbs Frederick	3	[illegible]	No Pay	Temporary Boy [illegible]

When Mr. Neville talks of the cylinders being lagged, presumably he means the covers, as Mr. Arnott says. In either case lagging, by retaining the heat, should improve rather than worsen performance, even though the improvement would be negligible on inside cylinders. Inclined cylinders tend to make a locomotive "shoulder" at starting, but will not affect its performance at speed; otherwise the Gresley "Pacifics," with their steeply inclined inside cylinders, would be unsatisfactory machines.

The "Experiments" were not as good as the "Precursors". They were often mishandled by the firemen, for their fireboxes were shallower and they had to be fired differently from the "Precursors" and "Jubilees". Also, they were prone to slip at speed without any visible cause - (they are one of the few classes known to slip with the regulator shut).

But their real fault was that they could not be thrashed like the "Precursors" and "Jumbos". A "Precursor" could and did take 440-ton trains regularly to Crewe and Carlisle too - and "Jumbos" sometimes had to stand in for them! No other railway had to take such loads as were normal on the L. & N.W.R.; 13-16 coach trains were the order of the day, and they took some pulling. Given a train of 12 coaches or under, the "Experiments" did very well. They were lighter on coal than the "Precursors" and also light on repairs. But when they were metamorphosed into the "Princes" they were twice as good. The "Princes" would tackle anything, and would steam like kettles - in short, they could be thrashed unmercifully and seemed to enjoy it.

Mr. Arnott cannot remember 80 m.p.h. on the L. & N.W.R., mainly for the reason that neither the timetables nor the loads usually permitted such a speed. But I remember over 85 m.p.h. on several occasions - on the 3.55 a.m. Crewe-London when running down from Berkhamsted to Euston: we wanted our breakfast!

Yours faithfully,

KENNETH CANTLIE.

Eaton Square, S.W.1.

27th July 1950.

Finch, William Thomas – 'Bill'. LNWR Society Member and Model Builder Extraordinary.

By Richard Foster

Bill Finch was born in Aston, Birmingham, on 12th April 1906. Attendance at metalwork classes at the age of 12 started a lifetime of model building. He left school at 14 and was apprenticed as a machinist to Wolseley Motors (then part of Vickers). His walk to work alongside the Birmingham to Coventry line cemented a life-long love of the LNWR – usually trains hauled by 'Experiments', 'Princes', 'Precursors', 'Cauliflowers' and 'Coal Tanks' would pass! Later jobs included a mouldmaker at GEC and toolmaker at Joseph Lucas, and toolroom foreman at Midland Electrical Manufacturing Co. Ltd.

He was a founder member of the Birmingham Society of Model Engineers and became interested in making an accurate model of an LNWR engine. He chose a 'Jumbo' as being the most suitable in terms of looks and size – he had decided on a scale of 1 and 1/16th inch to the foot. The frames of the locomotive *Miranda* were laid down in 1946 and the job was finally finished in 1971 – his retirement year!

One of the reasons for the long construction period was the need to undertake detailed research, obtaining drawings and information on the prototype. He was able to borrow drawings from Crewe and where details were missing, measured up details on some existing and preserved LNWR locomotives. As a result he ended up with sketch books full of locomotive details.

Bill was a member of the LNWRS from its formation in 1973 until his death in January 1999. In order to bring his wonderful sketches to a wider audience and make them available for other researchers and model builders, the Society published *The Bill Finch Portfolio* (Premier Portfolio No. 14) in 1999 (since republished

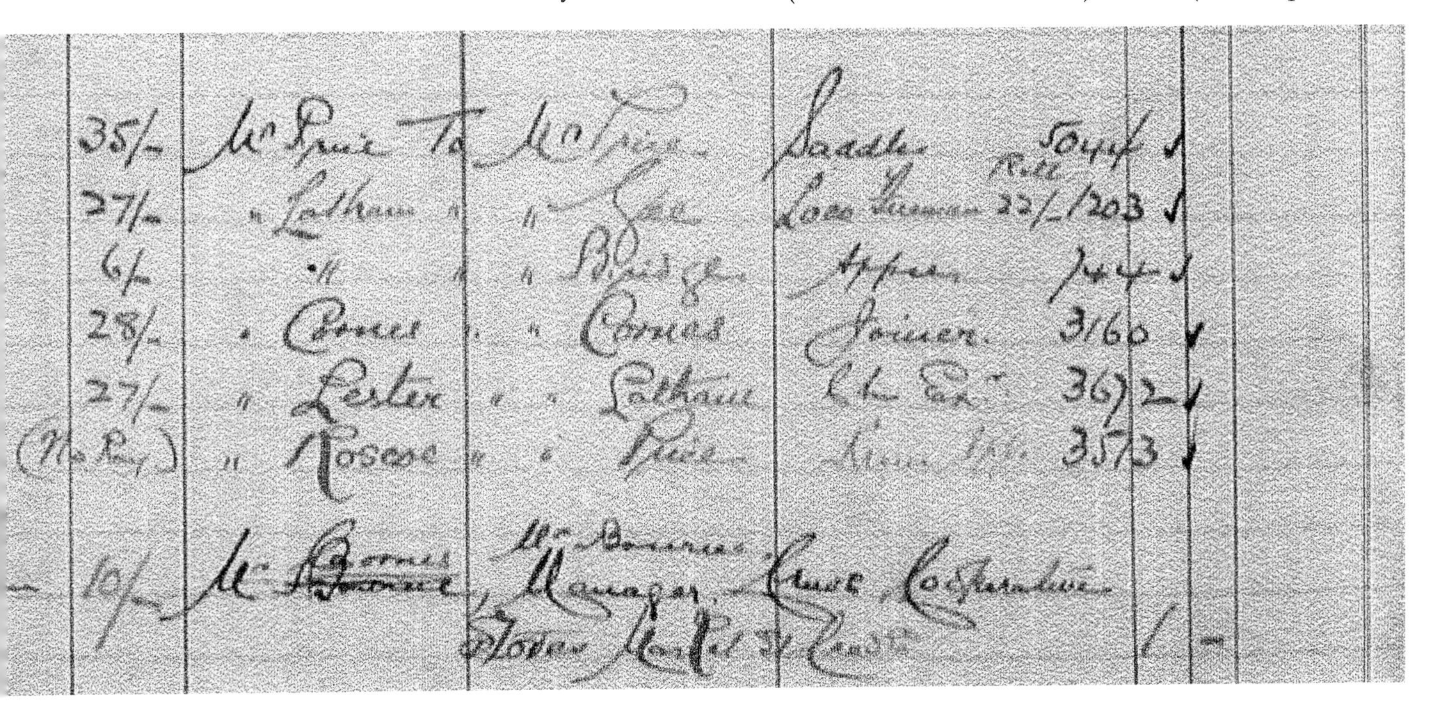

35/-	Mr Price	To	Mr Price	Saddler	5046
27/-	" Latham	"	" [illegible]	[illegible]	22/1203
6/-	"	"	" Bridge	[illegible]	144
28/-	" Jones	"	" Jones	Joiner	3160
27/-	" Lester	"	" Latham	[illegible]	3672
(No Pay)	" Roscoe	"	" Price	[illegible]	3573
10/-	Mr Barnes		Mr Barnes Manager, [illegible]		1/-

as *Building a London & North Western Railway Jumbo: The Bill Finch Portfolio of Locomotive Details.* It includes further details of Bill and his activities and hence the notes here have been kept brief (see also page 17).

Fisher, Patrick John.
Successor to G P Neele, LNWR Superintendent of the Line, LNWR Society Member, Society President 1980-1. **By Richard Foster**

Patrick Fisher was born in Hong Kong on 25th May 1909, the son of Henry George C Fisher and Jessie Marion Fisher (nee Connar), who had been married in Paddington, London, in 1908. The Connar family came from Liverpool, while the Fisher family came from Northampton, where Henry's father, John, was a machinist in the shoe trade. Henry was the third son and became a commercial clerk, initially in Northampton but later he moved about, including overseas, and was presumably in Hong Kong on business when Patrick was born.

Henry seems to have done well for himself, and Patrick was well spoken and probably public school educated. He was a career railwayman and by the beginning of World War 2 was a Train Controller at Rugby. When the war started he told me that he desperately wanted to join the forces and do his bit, but he was in a reserved occupation and railway management would not let him go. He thus found the war period rather frustrating. Management on the other hand probably realised that they desperately needed people like him if the railways were going to be kept going and war-time traffic dealt with in difficult conditions. However Patrick was not entirely confined to Britain and is recorded as travelling from Port Harcourt, Nigeria to Liverpool in April 1943.

After the war he was progressively promoted, becoming Divisional Operating Superintendent, Western Division, London Midland Region, in the early part of 1957. This was effectively the equivalent of the LNWR 'Superintendent of the Line' post, occupied by G P Neele for many years. 'P J Fisher' will be very familiar to anyone who has studied LMR timetables and operating documents as the name appeared on many Working Timetables and working documents over his period in office.

In 1961 he transferred to the West Coast Electrification Project, and among other things had responsibility for the redesign of the track, platform and signalling layout at Euston, being appointed Co-ordinating Officer Euston Reconstruction. He said that the brief was to make the main line platforms as long as possible and provide sufficient capacity to accommodate all the Midland Main Line trains so that St Pancras could be closed. He commented that the final layout achieved this, though rather tight, but top management had failed to realise how much passenger traffic would grow once the electric services started. So, within a few years the capacity set aside for the Midland had largely been used up.

As an LMR senior officer he was based at Euston and lived in a large house in a leafy part of Haslemere in Surrey. It appears that a large proportion of the Euston-based management of the LMS and LMR lived in Surrey. I have heard it said that the services into Euston would have been rather better had more of the management lived north of London! Patrick participated in the periodic officers' inspections of the region's network, often by means of an Officers' Special Train. He once told me that in the case of any inspection in the West Cumberland area, the timetable of the Officers' Special was always written around a long lunch stop at Bassenthwaite Lake. While the Officers were busy in the nearby hotel, the train crew knew they had a lengthy period in which to do their own thing!

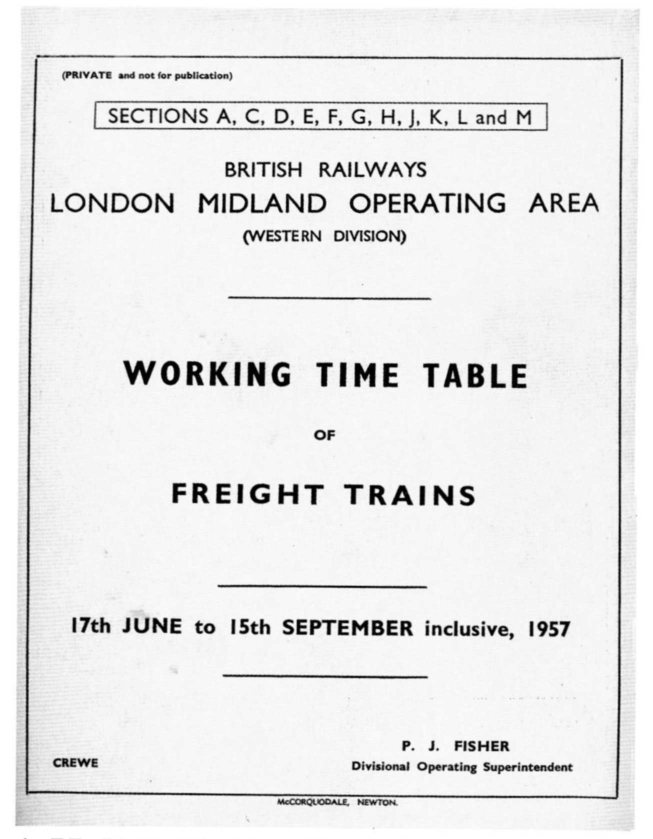
(PRIVATE and not for publication)

SECTIONS A, C, D, E, F, G, H, J, K, L and M

BRITISH RAILWAYS
LONDON MIDLAND OPERATING AREA
(WESTERN DIVISION)

WORKING TIME TABLE
OF
FREIGHT TRAINS

17th JUNE to 15th SEPTEMBER inclusive, 1957

CREWE

P. J. FISHER
Divisional Operating Superintendent

McCORQUODALE, NEWTON.

A BR LMR Working Timetable cover from the period when Patrick was Divisional Operating Superintendent.

After his retirement Patrick took an active part in Society affairs, attending a number of meetings and 'at-homes'. Indeed he arranged one at his own home, which Huw Edwards and I, among others, attended. After years of commuting, Patrick knew the walking time from front door to station platform to the nearest few seconds, so if his train was on time, he and the train would arrive at the platform at the same moment! He introduced me to Peter Shute, who had been Chief Signal Engineer, West Coast Modernisation (the 1958-67 one!). As well as telling me tales of the resignalling he remarked 'Control areas are getting bigger all the time. In a few years it should be possible to control the whole railway network from one's office'. Talk about far-sightedness, this was several years before the invention of the Personal Computer, let alone its appearance on office desks and in people's homes. Network Rail hope to get down to a small number of regional control centres in the 2020s!

Patrick also attended an 'at-home' at my home in Sutton Coldfield. I met him again soon after, when he started the conversation with 'After I left your house to go home by train I got caught short'. This seemed an odd thing to say, and I wondered what was coming next! He continued 'Yes, I found that my whisky bottle was empty, so I had to stop off at Euston to get new supplies. Fortunately the restaurant still had some bottles of BR's own-brand 'Royal Scot' whisky, so I was alright for the rest of the journey!'

Yours sincerely,
Patrick J. Elder.

Signature from letter.

During his time in control at Rugby, he found an old District Occurrence book from the early days. He spent some time abstracting the more interesting entries, some of which he submitted for inclusion in *Premier News*. I seem to remember one entitled 'Tigers on the Line, trains stopped'. Another is reproduced below. Patrick was elected Society President for the year 1980-1 and died in July 2000.

Collision between Birmingham Mail and a cattle train at Leamington Junction, Rugby 16th December 1860.

The policeman's box, which is a large wooden structure about 10 feet square, on the front of which stand two high signal posts, having a platform 16 or 20 feet high. The hut was thrown down the embankment into the adjoining field, a distance of some 50 feet. Strange to say, the policeman, who was in the box, and was thrown down with it, was unhurt. 'No lives were lost'.

Perhaps this is why the LNWR opted for substantial brick-built signal cabins!

Flegg, Jeremy William
Founder Member, LNWR Society, and Society Benefactor.

By Richard Foster

Jeremy Flegg was born in Chislehurst, Kent, on 12th September 1942, and began his working life with the Royal Exchange Group in Beckenham as an Insurance Clerk. In 1970 he and his parents moved to Burgess Hill after he took a job in Brighton with the newly-formed Guardian Royal Exchange. He remained there until 1990 when he transferred to Croydon before taking early retirement in 1996. Outside of work and his more formal duties, he devoted his life to studying Greek, heraldry, railway history, model railways and classical music.

Following the death of his father around 1990 he joined Burgess Hill's United Reformed Church, eventually becoming a church elder. He was secretary of Brighton's Insurance Institute for 25 years and was made honorary secretary of the Southern Regional Forum in 1999. He continued to live in the modest bungalow in Burgess Hill after his parents died and until his own death.

He was a founder member of the LNWR Society, and attended several of our early meetings, possibly including the inaugural ones in 1973. He listed his interests as 1900-1923 locomotives and rolling stock, signalling and train services. He made some contributions to *Premier News*, including occasional book reviews.

He died in the Royal Marsden Hospital in the spring of 2001 at the early age of 58, after a short battle with leukaemia. He left behind an estate worth £677,225 which was shared between ten charities, mostly concerned with animals or railways. Friends described him as eccentric, quiet and polite and were surprised at how much money he left. One said: 'He was the kind of chap you always felt you had to buy the drinks for - it was just the way he was.' A former colleague said: 'I am quite amazed at that amount but I knew he had a head for the stock market. He was unfailingly courteous and a true gentleman.' The Reverend Andrew Fairchild, minister of the URC where Mr Flegg sang and preached, said: 'He was a very faithful member of the church, he was very well read and he was exceptionally well educated. But he was never arrogant and was a great loss to the life of the church.'

Among his bequests was one which amounted £43,291.59 to the LNWR Society. Of this £25,000 was paid in April 2002, and the balance in August 2004 after allowing for expenses, taxes etc. This was placed in a separate fund to be spent on special projects. Some of the money was used to help set up our Archive and Study Centre in Kenilworth and the remainder of the money is being used to help fund the purchase of additional archive material.

The Society owes Jeremy a huge debt of gratitude for his generous bequest, which has been of immense value in creating our Study Centre and developing and expanding our archive. In recognition of this the Study Centre was named *The Jeremy Flegg Study Centre*.

Fraser, Neil.
Railway Observer, Historian and Writer,
Member LNWR Historical Society,
Founder Member LNWR Society,
President LNWR Society 2000-2001.
By Richard Foster

Neil Fraser was born on 15th April 1925 and lived all his life, other than National Service, in the Huddersfield area. His main interests mainly dated from school days, primarily railways but also rugby league and cricket. Serious railway observations started at school; he learnt that the daily goods train on the Midland branch into Huddersfield Newtown passed near his school at lunchtime and regularly went out to observe it. Late running led to a late return and reprimands from time to time.

He enlisted in the Royal Mechanical and Electrical Engineers in 1943, where he regarded his war and national service as the holiday of a lifetime and made the most of it. He made a point of visiting railway installations wherever he went - France, Belgium and Germany during the war and soon after, and later Palestine and Egypt. He seems to have retained his interests in the railways he visited after his return to civilian life, and wrote an article on the Hedjaz-Jordan Railway Locomotives in the SLS Journal in 1965.

After demobilisation in 1947 he returned to Huddersfield, married Kathleen Wright in 1951 and raised two daughters Rowena & Ros. He worked as a foundryman for 25 years and then for a few years as a market trader until illness forced him into early retirement in 1982. He became a magistrate in the 1970s, serving on the bench for 25 years. He said that he found the experience deeply satisfying and very often enjoyable, while he had learnt a lot about life from it!

Neil took an interest in all forms of transport and wrote many articles for railway and waterways journals. He also contributed regularly to his local newspaper, the *Huddersfield Examiner*. He was a founder member of the Huddersfield Railway Circle when it was formed in 1947 and a past Chairman, and also a long-standing member of the Stephenson Locomotive Society (he joined in 1958) and a regular attendee at their meetings in Manchester. He was a founder member of the LNWR Historical Society when it was formed in 1962, and wrote several papers for it. He joined the LNWR Society on its formation and wrote a number of articles for *Premier News* and the *Journal*.

Railways ran in his blood. Neil's grandfather, Ben Garner, was a driver for the LNWR and LMS at Huddersfield (Hillhouse) shed between 1887 and 1925. As a result Neil had a deep affection for the shed and visited it at least weekly, often accompanied by his younger brother, Ian, especially if he had heard there was something unusual to see. On one occasion they found the Lickey banker '9F' 2-10-0, complete with headlight, on the Crewe goods, which was used as a running in turn from the Works.

In the early 1980s he suffered the first of several heart attacks. As his health gradually worsened, his pace of life inevitably had to become slower, and the number of pills he had to take larger, but his writing output continued. He published his first book *Hillhouse Immortals* about his favourite locomotive shed in 1999. This featured the reminiscences of his many railwaymen friends and material from the diaries of Ben Garner. One of Neil's favourite stories concerned Harry Eastwood, a local driver. One day after Harry's train arrived at Huddersfield, non-stop from Stalybridge, a gentleman wearing a top hat and frock coat emerged out of the steam and smoke. He took out his gold watch and exclaimed that the schedule allowed 21 minutes and the train had just done it in 19! Harry responded 'That's nowt – yesterday I did it in 18 and a half!' It was said that the gentleman was F W Webb.

Neil was always willing to help others; Harry Jack remembers long correspondences with him on various LNWR subjects (they had originally met on the footbridge at Crewe station - both observing trains!). In recognition of his achievements and contribution to the Society Neil was elected LNWR Society President in 2000.

Neil died on 28th March 2001. Graham Hardy gave a short tribute on behalf of his railway friends at the funeral service at Huddersfield Crematorium, after which there was a short period of reflection with a background of steam locomotive sounds. His ashes were scattered on the old LNWR at Paddock Cutting near his home.

(With thanks to Ian Fraser, Graham Hardy and Harry Jack)

Nix, Denis John - Denis.
Railway Modeller and Writer,
Long Standing LNWR Society Member,
Committee Member, Treasurer 1987-2000,
Vice-President 2000-7. **By Bob Williams**

Denis & Joyce Nix at the bowling club. Denis is in characteristic pose and the pipe and the yellow stain to the moustache are evident, but on this occasion the smoke is absent! (Courtesy Geoff Nix)

Denis John Nix was born in 1925 at Tunbridge Wells in Kent. He attended Friern Barnet school and on leaving joined the National Provincial Bank, Boreham Wood, in 1942. He was called up to the Army in 1943 and joined the RAOC where he served in France, Belgium and Germany before demobilisation in 1947. He returned to the National Provincial Bank and worked in various branches in London and Middlesex before his retirement as branch manager (as they were in those days!) of the Harefield branch. He married Joyce in 1945 and they had two sons, Raymond and Geoffrey. Whilst dedicated to being a family man, his wife was often subject to being a railway enthusiasts 'widow'.

Prior to his conversion to railway modelling he constructed working model boats and aircraft which his sons also took to for several years. Not being sentimental about his work, at least one beautiful scale working paddle steamer was cannibalised during the construction of a large railway layout in the loft of the Chorleywood family home!

Denis became well known to modellers in the 1960s through his regular appearances in the demonstration area (nicknamed 'the cage') at the Model Railway Club's Easter Exhibition at Central Hall, Westminster. His brushed back white hair and handlebar moustache were instantly recognisable through the haze of smoke from his pipe. Although he was a prolific scratch builder in '00' scale, his models at that time were not exceptional. He modelled LNWR locos, carriages and wagons, but most of the early carriages had the panelling drawn on. He did do quite a lot of research and some of his carriage drawings appeared in the modelling press of the day. He had a healthy sense of humour about his hobby and jointly authored a spoof modelling article describing a 'Protoscale Society' in the model railway press.

Over the next 40 years Denis produced better and better models to the extent that many of his later models were of almost professional quality with painting and lining to match. I remember a particularly fine scratch built '00' 'Claughton' which he built despite a whitemetal kit being available; this was his second 'Claughton', the first being the subject of a demonstration in 'the cage' in the 1960s. He also moved partially into 7mm where he produced some

Denis's model of 2-4-0 860 *Merrie Carlisle*. The LNWR engine was an 'Improved Precedent' or 'Large Jumbo' built in November 1894 to replace a 'Precedent' of 1877. The loco became LMS 5050 and was scrapped in 1933. (Courtesy Geoff Nix)

beautiful models, some from modified kits and some completely scratch built. We know Denis for his LNWR models but he was also an LSWR and Isle of Wight enthusiast producing most of the models for the *Bembridge* layout in '00'. Living in Chorleywood, he was an active member of his local model railway club for many years, and a member of the Historical Model Railway Society.

Denis was always happy to talk to and help fellow modellers in his own modest way, perhaps using the skills from his job as a bank manager. He shared a lifetime hobby of crown bowls with his wife, being a committee member of his local club for many years. Denis was Treasurer of the LNWR Society for many years and some years after he started I was appointed as Examiner. When he decided to step down I became Treasurer and later Denis became examiner of my work, role reversals or 'poachers and gamekeepers' indeed! Denis died in August 2007 at the age of 83.

(With grateful thanks to Geoff Nix)

A Personal Comment from Peter Stanton:

I had been aware of Denis for many years; he was one of the names that regularly appeared in the modelling magazines. I looked back on some of these articles. His work was still fresh and adventurous all those years after it was written and I learned again at the hand of one of the masters of the hobby.

Platt, Geoffrey Hine – Geoff or GH, M.Sc. (Tech), M.I.E.E.
Authority on the LNWR, long-standing Member of the Society, and its first Speaker. President of the Historical Model Railway Society and Vice-President of the Manchester Model Railway Society. By Richard Foster

Geoffrey Hine Platt was born in Chorlton, Manchester on 28th March 1910. He was the son of William Platt, a commercial traveller in the wholesale sugar trade and Florence Annie Platt (nee Hine, hence his middle name) who had been married for two years. They lived in Demesne Road, Alexandra Park, sharing the house with Annie Hine, Mother-in-Law and Ruth Griffith, servant. He married Kathleen M Crees in 1936. Geoff joined the SLS in 1943 when his address was The Parsonage, Hatherlow, Romiley, but he moved to Whiteleafe, Surrey, in 1949 and later moved to Purley. He became a lecturer in electrical engineering at the University of London, and spoke with considerable authority on the subject.

Geoff Platt was one of the leading authorities on the LNWR, ranking with J P Richards in his knowledge and willingness to share it. He gave many lectures and talks on LNWR subjects. He took many photographs of ex-LNWR subjects from the 1930s and even travelled around with Jim on field trips from time to time. One enthusiast from the period recalled arriving at a steam shed one Sunday to find two men in raincoats equipped with tape measures, rulers and notebooks clambering all over a Webb 2-4-2 tank, much to the bemusement of the shed staff. The gentlemen were Messrs Platt and Richards in action. The observer remarked 'it occurred to me how little we perhaps realise the trouble they go to in order to ensure accuracy in drawings and models'.

Geoff was a very good draughtsman and several of his drawings appeared in the *Model Railway Constructor* from the late 1930s along with some fine detailed photographs. He was also a fine modeller in 7mm/1ft scale, and some of his models were displayed at some of the Society's early meetings and the exhibition at Crewe Grammar School.

Geoff's particular gift was his willingness to help other enthusiasts and nothing ever seemed to be too much trouble. He would go to extraordinary lengths to help, providing copies of photographs and other information. Letters from him often contained sketches to set out and explain details. In those early days he was one of the few photographers to record items of infrastructure, signals and lineside equipment. As a result many of his photographs were unique.

Geoff was a leading light in the Model Railway Club, the Manchester Model Railway Society and the Historical Model Railway Society, and gave our own Society considerable encouragement in its early years.

There was a down side to all the helpfulness and participation. Because of the time he spent helping others his own published output was relatively small. After his death, Kathleen Platt told me that probably her greatest regret about Geoff was that he had not put his great knowledge to use in the publication of his own books, which would have been a lasting tribute to him. In this context it is interesting to see the comments of Philip Millard elsewhere in this publication.

At the time of his death Geoff was working on a definitive work, an LNWR *'Livery Register'* for the HMRS. This work was taken on and completed by Edward Talbot, Philip Millard, George Dow and Peter Davis. The book, published in 1985, included the following in its dedication to Geoff:

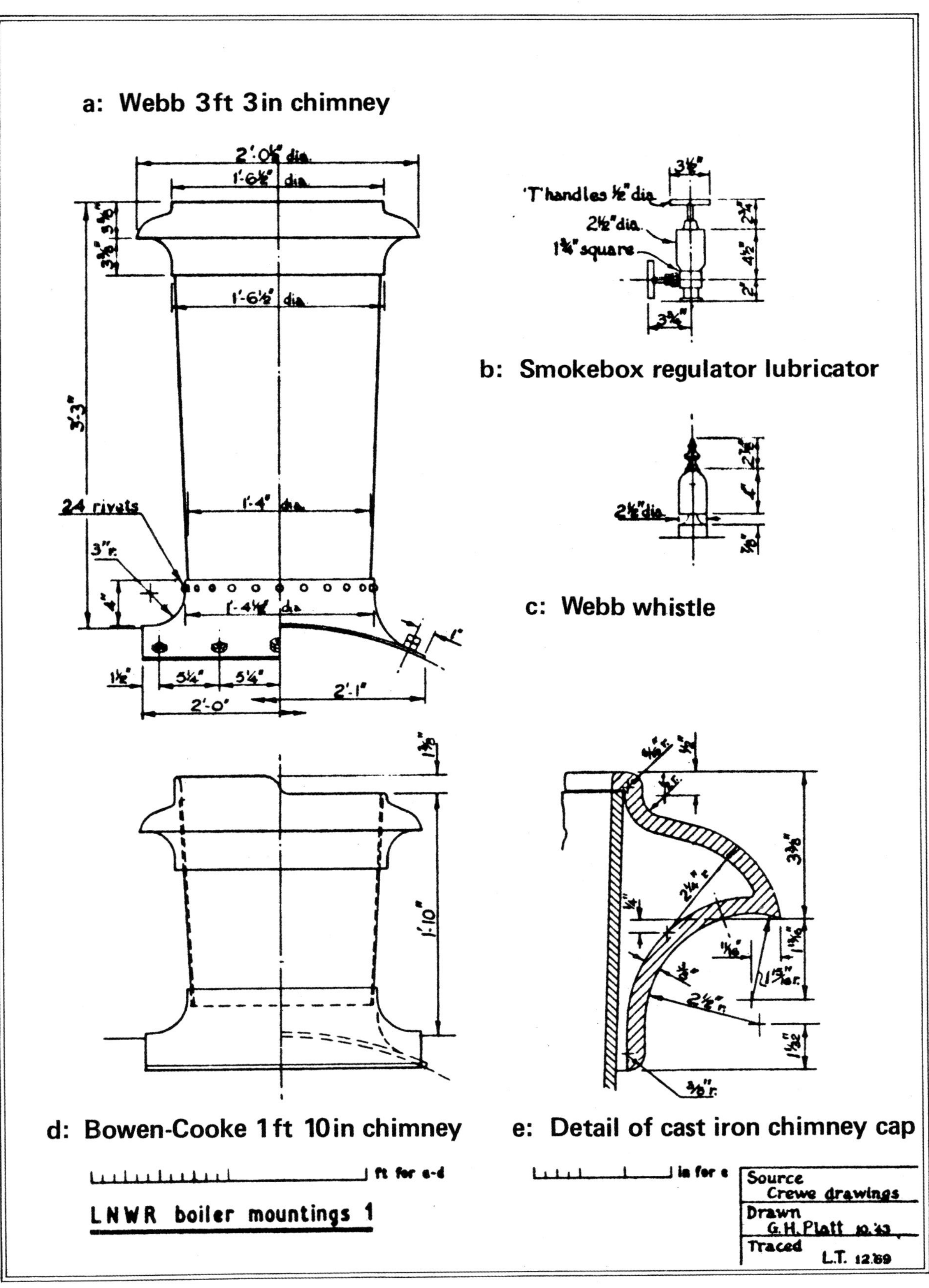

One of Geoff Platt's drawings, showing locomotive chimney details.

'Geoffrey Platt, to whom this book is dedicated, died on 25th July 1980. For nearly 20 years he was Sub-Dean of the Faculty of Engineering at King's College, London University. He joined the HMRS soon after its foundation in 1950 and became devoted to its interests. He served continuously on its Executive Committee, with a break of only two years, from 1955 until his retirement in 1975, occupying successively the posts of Secretary, Deputy Chairman in 1963 and Chairman in 1972.'

When he retired in 1975, he moved to Holywell in North Wales, providing even more help to fellow enthusiasts. Geoff died suddenly from a massive heart attack in July 1980 at the early age of 70 while he was working on an operating session at Ken Longbottom's huge 0 gauge garden layout.

Geoff was hugely helpful to me while I was researching and writing *LNWR Signalling*. He gave freely of his time in reading and commenting on drafts of the manuscript and provided me with copies of a lot of his own signal photographs which greatly helped in understanding LNWR practice. A number of his photographs were used in the book. My great regret was that he did not live long enough to see it published.

A personal appreciation by Bob Williams

Geoff was a true gentleman and a big influence on my father. In fact, although my father didn't have a middle name, the HMRS registered him as G H Williams which he never corrected as I believe he liked the association! He also helped me with career discussions during my 'A' levels, based on his own professional experiences. He played the important role of Liaison Officer at the famous Model Railway Easter Exhibitions at Central Hall Westminster, whilst his wife could often be found selling tickets to the thousands queuing to get in. It was a real family affair as Geoff had two sons (Michael and Ron) and Ron was part of the team building the huge *Longridge, Brampton Sands and Calshott* 4mm layout which appeared at the same show for several years.

Rayner, Eric.
LNWR Society Founder and First President 1975-8.

By Richard Foster

Eric Rayner was born in the Manchester area on 23rd January 1920, and was a life-long LNWR enthusiast. He said that he did not have the knowledge or skills to undertake research of his own. His health also precluded many activities. He had had tuberculosis as a youth which had damaged his lungs and collapsed his chest, which made breathing difficult and affected his heart. Eric married Kathleen Cockcroft in Stockport in the summer of 1950.

He was an engineer and had his own workshop where he built internal combustion engines and indulged in aero modelling. He installed radio control in a 5 inch gauge steam locomotive model at a time when such things were in their infancy.

After he retired he realised that what was needed was a society to bring people with interests in the LNWR together. This would allow knowledge to be shared, and help people to find information and share their enthusiasm. Early in 1973 he put out circulars and adverts to try and bring together interested people, and arranged meetings in Crewe in July and September 1973 at which it was decided to form a Society. Although he became the first Chairman he always said he felt he could contribute very little and wanted to learn about the LNWR from others. His contributions were in getting the Society started and through his subscriptions helping to provide the means of bringing people together and disseminating information.

At some point I came across one of his preliminary notes, and although I had missed the first meeting I wrote to him and received an invitation to go and see him, which I did at the end of July 1973. He lived in a large rambling house in Heaton Moor. The house was used as a nursing home for the elderly, which was Kathleen's business, with Eric as the help and handyman, often preparing the meals. He and Kathleen were a very kind and homely couple and I stayed there over several weekends over the next couple of years, these sometimes coinciding with Society meetings!

Unfortunately Eric suffered bouts of ill-health and severe migraine attacks which increased in frequency as time progressed and he had to miss several of the Society meetings, which must have come very hard after he had gone to so much trouble to get the Society set up. He died of a heart attack on 18th March 1978.

Workmen's Trains – a bygone era.

Eric told me once that in his early working days jobs were rather scarce and at one time the only thing he could find was a job in Huddersfield. This involved daily travel from the family home in Stockport. Cost of travel was a significant issue, and the only way he could make it work was to travel very early using cheap workmen's tickets. These had considerable conditions attached to stop use by the better-off, and were only available for local journeys. The nearest he could get to Huddersfield was Stalybridge, although tickets were available from there to Huddersfield. This led to a daily ritual. Each day, as his train ran into Stalybridge, doors all along the train opened and men would be out onto the platform running alongside the train before it had come to a stand! This was followed by a thunderous race down the subway ramp to the booking office where a queue quickly formed. After buying the new ticket it was a case of running as quickly as possible back up the ramp in the hope of getting back onto the platform before the Huddersfield train departed!

Rouet, Paul.
LNWR Society Member, Drawings Officer 1991-2009, Society Chairman 1992-2004.
By Roy Thomson

Paul was born in Manchester in 1937. His father was Swiss born and in business in North Manchester as a Baker and Pâtissier. Paul's local railways included former LNWR & L&YR lines and he took an interest in both. As a schoolboy, family holidays were spent on the North Wales coast and it was there he really came under the 'Premier Line' spell. He liked variety, however, and used to say how thrilled he was as a boy with trips to Golborne to visit family friends. These trips involved running over the CLC from Manchester Central and the former GCR St. Helens branch from Glazebrook.

He worked for IBM, and for some years he was based in the USA. While there he and his wife Carol lived in Connecticut. He became very fond of the country and I think he would have liked to have settled there. Following their return to the UK they took their annual holidays in the US and drove all over the country, even getting to the West Coast and down to New Orleans. He had a great ambition to travel on Route 66 from Chicago to Los Angeles and they managed to do this shortly before he died.

After 12 years of hard work Paul Rouet retired from the post of Society Chairman at the 2004 AGM. To mark the occasion, and as a small 'thank you' from the Society, the incoming Chairman, Peter Stanton, presented Paul (right) with an LNWR crest.

Paul spent a lot of time in researching his family history on his mother's side, who were from Lancashire (her maiden name was Ashworth). Paul expressed his railway interests by making a start on an LMS 4mm model railway with motive power provided by LMS and former LNWR locos and a mix of LNWR and L&YR coaching stock. Sadly the layout was incomplete at the time of his death in May 2009. Of the LMS types, he was particularly fond of the Stanier Class Five mixed traffic engines. He was very interested in collieries and particularly in their private-owner wagons and those of coal merchants. He had a fondness for Point of Ayr Colliery and the Mostyn Iron Works and the harbour there.

In the Society, his first post was as Drawings Officer into which he made a splendid job of listing and microfilming the ever growing number of drawings which came into the Society's possession. When I wanted to stand down from the Chairmanship in 1992 I asked Paul if he would take it on and fortunately he agreed. He became a popular Chairman whose friendly and conscientious approach served the Society well as both Chairman and Drawings Officer.

Paul was a very kind person and would help anyone in all sorts of ways. I called on him from time to time and he always gave me a great welcome and made a point of showing me the latest railway book he had bought. It was a sad day when he told me liver cancer had been diagnosed. He seemed to accept that he hadn't long to live. This was to be the case and despite treatment he only lasted a few weeks after. He died comparatively young, and it is a great pity that he isn't still around for us to enjoy his company and for him to enjoy his interests.

Weaver, Colin Rodney – 'Rodney'.
Engineering and Locomotive Historian, Model Engineer, Long-Standing LNWR Society Member and Society President 2002-3.
By Richard Foster

Rodney Weaver was born on 23rd November 1939 in Bristol. He was educated at Bablake School, Coventry, and Imperial College, London, where he read chemical engineering. Following graduation he worked for the Blue Circle Cement Company until 1962, when he went to Bristol Siddley Engines (later Rolls Royce), at the old Armstrong Siddley works in Coventry. He remained there until 1999 when he took early retirement. He was always enthusiastic about his work, which he clearly knew in intimate detail.

Rodney had a deep understanding of engineering history and was a prolific contributor to many historical railway journals and magazines. His book, *Baguley Locomotives 1914-1931* was published in 1975, followed by *Steam on Canals*, co-authored with his father, Phillip, whose own specialism was canals. Both books are regarded as classics in their field.

Rodney had a great interest in narrow gauge railways and travelled extensively, recording systems in France, Portugal, Switzerland, Italy, Ireland and Wales. In North Wales he discovered a lost Baguley petrol engine No 774, stored in an old slate mill at the Oakley Quarries. He promptly bought it for preservation. He was an active supporter of the Festiniog Railway, spending part of his annual holidays working as a locomotive fireman. He designed and built *Minim* a 7¼inch gauge single Fairlie locomotive. This was a 'ride-on' machine, with full cab protection, incorporating such things as Palmer flexible steam pipes, polypropylene water tanks and his annular blast pipe.

In 1994 Rodney approached the National Railway Museum to suggest that they mounted a small exhibition to mark the bicentenary of Edward Bury's birth. Harry Jack remembers accompanying him on a visit to make the proposal, but Rodney made a strong case on his own and the NRM undertook to do something. Rodney wrote the NRM leaflet to accompany the display.

Rodney joined the LNWRS in about 1984, and was a regular attendee at meetings, usually bringing along his father, latterly in a wheelchair. He would soon be deep in conversation with someone. He contributed a number of articles to *Premier News* and the *Journal*.

Rodney was always enthusiastic, willingly sharing his encyclopaedic knowledge with others. Harry Jack recalls long correspondences and telephone calls, while Gordon Webster recalled that he was always a pleasure to be with, enjoying a good debate and could always lift a flagging conversation. He loved the Goons and was a fine mimic; his take-off of Harold Wilson was brilliant. He had a sharp wit and could be hilarious when the occasion arose. Ken Wood summed Rodney up when he described him succinctly as a 'practical theorist'. He died on 6th January 2003.

(With thanks to Gordon Webster and Harry Jack.)

Whitworth, Gordon Dudley – 'Dudley' or 'GD', (never Gordon).
LNWR Historical Society and LNWR Society Founder Member, Chairman LNWRHS, LNWRS Treasurer 1973-1981, President 1981-2, Vice-President 1983-1988.

By Richard Foster

Dudley Whitworth was born on 29th October 1914 and was a life-long railway enthusiast. His first love was the LNWR, with the CLC and MSJ&A following up. His primary interest was locomotives, and much of his time was devoted to finding and recording details of LNWR locomotives, and over his lifetime he built up a huge collection of information and photographs.

By profession Dudley was a railwayman, working for the LMS and BR in the Manchester district. He lived all his life in the Altrincham area, so must have built up a staggering number of 'daily commute' journeys over the MSJ&A!

He was a close friend of Bertram Baxter, who collected information on all locomotives, which he recorded on a card index which eventually amounted to over 40,000 cards. Dudley was custodian of the index for a while after Bertram's death. The core of the information was published in *British Locomotive Catalogue 1825-1923*, Edited by David Baxter and published by Moorland Publishing Company from 1978. Volumes 2A & 2B covered the LNWR.

Dudley was very friendly and always willing to share his knowledge of the LNWR, and was one of life's gentlemen. He was an active member of a number of societies, including the Manchester, Stephenson and Industrial Locomotive Societies. He joined the SLS in 1951 and was on the Committee for many years. He was Chairman and Editor of the LNWR Historical Society during its short existence and Treasurer and Membership Secretary of the LNWRS for many years, being elected President on his 'retirement'.

In 1959 he married Florence M Burt, who was born in Liverpool in September 1930. In later years he bought one of the railwaymen's cottages (built 1859) at Low Gill Junction on the Lancaster & Carlisle Railway and spent many happy times there.

After his death on 3rd July 1988, age 73, the Society produced *LNWR One Man's Passion – A Tribute to G.D. Whitworth* – Premier Portfolio No 9 in 1991. This featured a number of his pieces on a variety of locomotive subjects. It also contains information on Dudley and his work, and so the notes here have been kept brief. Material from his collection was donated to the Society Archive.

Geoff Williams working on his *Aylesbury* layout. The passenger station is in the left distance, with the loco shed and goods shed on the right. His gas works model later occupied the place where he is working.
(Courtesy Mike Williams)

Williams, Geoffrey – 'Geoff'. Creator of 'Aylesbury', LNWRS Member, Secretary 1981-8, President 1993-8.

By Bob and Mike Williams

Geoff was born in April 1913 and was interested in railways from an early age. Although he was born in GER territory in Tottenham he liked the romance of the LNWR and its routes from Euston to exotic places like Carlisle and Holyhead. After leaving school he moved on to the usual girls and motorbikes and he was actually touring Germany on a motorbike when WW2 was declared!

Soon after the birth of his first son, Bob, in 1949, his railway interest was rekindled and he built his first 4mm freelance layout (to entertain his son of course!). This was LMS based but soon thoughts went back to the LNWR and in about 1956 he came across Aylesbury High Street station, which still kept many LNWR features including the station building with glass screen, signal box and loco shed, and appeared to be an attractive station to model.

He worked in EM but soon discovered that Aylesbury was much bigger than he thought with a goods shed and cattle dock behind the loco shed, so he started again with what he called *Aylesbury Mark 2.* This second model was as near to scale as space would allow and also used home-made 'finescale' soldered track using TT rail on plywood sleepers. He pioneered the use of 18.2mm gauge, which greatly improved running and appearance. *Aylesbury Mark 2* had a lever frame with electric locking between signals and points but, he never considered linking this to track current as he said a real engine driver could ignore signals if he wanted to!

Aylesbury Mark 1 was sold but most of the stock was retained, including his first scratch-built loco, a Chopper Tank. He bought the motor and wheels but made the rest. The inspiration for the model came from a 7mm model by Ross Pochin, and Ross supplied much information including some drawings.

Geoff's model of Aylesbury was unusual at the time in being a close model of an actual station, and this attention to detail continued with the stock which was largely built to portray what would have run to Aylesbury in pre-WW1 days, sometimes by modifying kits but often by scratch building. Later his love of building models meant that many 'unsuitable' models (e.g. 57ft toplight carriages) were added to the stock.

His thirst for historical information on Aylesbury and the LNWR led to friendships with many key figures at the time, including local ex-LNWR pensioners, coal merchants and others, but also J P Richards, Geoff Platt, Stan Garlick, Jack Nelson and many more. He joined the LNWR Society after encouragement from David Ratcliff (although he was at the inaugural meeting). He hosted a number of open days where visitors spent many happy hours with the layout or immersed in LNWR talk. His one regret was that he never kept a visitors book.

By profession he was a site engineer with Eastern Gas, so it was inevitable that the model of Aylesbury gas works would be particularly well detailed. His extensive researches into the Aylesbury Branch resulted in two large scrapbooks of letters, photographs, drawings, etc., and these played an important part in the production of the well-known book on the branch by Bill Simpson.

Geoff had three children. Bob and Mike retain their railway interest to this day but even Pete, the middle son, still owns a Reidpath LMS 4F and Ratio MR brake van from the early 50s layout. Geoff's wife, Beryl, always supported his hobby, providing tea and sandwiches at the open days and she still retains contact with some railway friends from those days. The current owner of *Aylesbury Mark 2* lives not far from Aylesbury and intends to put the model on the exhibition circuit. Geoff died in October 1998 at the age of 85.

Geoff Williams, an Appreciation, by Roy Thomson.

Geoff's working life was spent in the gas supply industry, except for wartime call-up to the Royal Navy where he served in minesweepers. Many of us first came across Geoff through his exceptional modelling skills. His *Aylesbury* model was well ahead of its time in terms of quality and detail and of such merit that it appeared on a number of occasions in the model railway press. Articles were published in the *MRN, Model Railways* and in the launch issue of *MRJ*. He was a member of the HMRS for over forty years.

Geoff was a kindly man and his way of life reflected his Christian principles. Sadly his last few years were spent in a wheelchair, much to his frustration. So keen was he to keep in touch with the running of the Society that, being unable to travel, he regularly invited the Committee to hold its meetings at his home in Cuffley. He retained his keen interest in railways and continued to construct models to the end. We can look back with great affection and admiration on a good man who achieved a great deal in his eighty-five years.

An excursion train approaching *Aylesbury*, no doubt reflecting Geoff's love of building carriages. The signal box is of size G with 30 levers and was built in 1882. A new station was constructed in 1889 on a new site to the south, hence the gap between box and tracks. At that date a full-size signal was provided for access to the goods yard (left-hand post as seen, the right-hand signal reads to the passenger station). In later years this was replaced by a ground signal. Note the standard LNWR iron footbridge. (Courtesy Mike Williams)

A view of part of the goods yard. The passenger station is off to the left, with the raised Platform Ground Frame behind the buffer stop at the foot of the platform ramp. The gas works is in place and dominates the area.
(Courtesy Mike Williams)

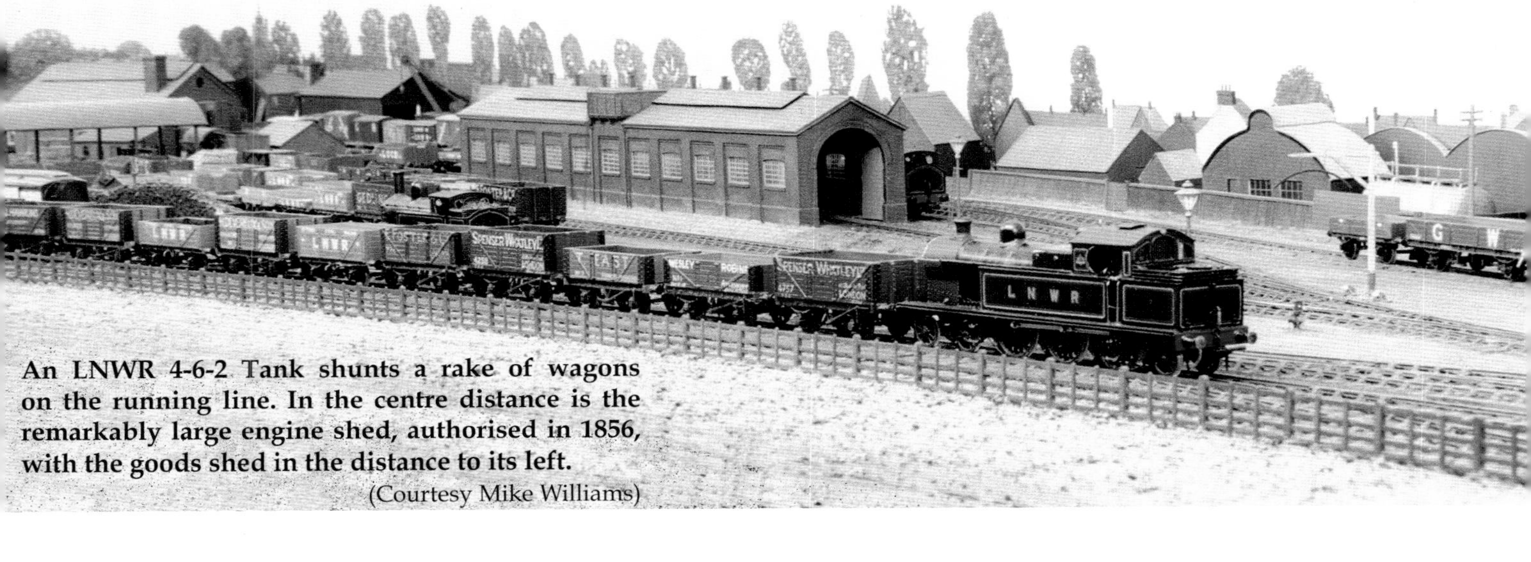

An LNWR 4-6-2 Tank shunts a rake of wagons on the running line. In the centre distance is the remarkably large engine shed, authorised in 1856, with the goods shed in the distance to its left.
(Courtesy Mike Williams)

The level crossing and signal box at Dropshort Street, with an 0-6-2 Tank resting between shunting duties. Note all the different types of fencing and gates reproducing the LNWR arrangements at Aylesbury, and the railway houses on the far side of the crossing. The perspective where the road disappears into the backscene is very effective.
(Courtesy Mike Williams)

APPENDIX - SOCIETY PUBLICATIONS

In addition to the Society members' magazine (The *Journal* and its predecessors), the Society has produced a large number of other publications, many of which have been detailed treatments of particular subjects. We have also published reprints of a number of interesting and historically valuable LNWR documents. Together these publications have now built up into an impressive and valuable archive of information on the LNWR. They are listed below as a record of what has been produced over the 40 years.

PREMIER PUBLICATION
The Friezland Accident of 1909, by M Smith. Published 1977, 8 pages, typewritten, card covers, 2 photographs and 2 plans.

PREMIER PORTFOLIOS
Between 1983 and 2004 our new publications were produced under the series title 'Premier Portfolios', a total of 16 titles were produced, some of which ran to second editions.

Premier Portfolio No 1 - Photograph and Drawing Miscellany. Published January 1983, 16 pages, compiled by David Clarke.

Premier Portfolio No 2 - Photograph and Drawing Miscellany. Published March 1983, 16 pages, compiled by David Clarke.

Premier Portfolio No 3 - The Locomotive Nameplates of the London & North Western Railway, by R Bell and E Talbot. Published January 1984, 18 pages.

Premier Portfolio No 4 - The Webb 'Experiment' Compounds, by C P Davis. Published February 1985, 38 pages.

Premier Portfolio No 5 - Crewe Works Narrow-Gauge System, by C S Taylor. Published June 1985, 18 pages. This booklet proved popular and quickly sold out. A second revised and much enlarged edition was published in 2005 (see below).

Premier Portfolio No 6 - The LNWR Bloomers, Wolverton's 7 ft Singles, by H Jack. Published December 1987, 30 pages. Cover price £2.50.

Premier Portfolio No 7 - Selected LNWR Carriages. A detailed commentary, by Philip A Millard. Published January 1989, 25 pages. Cover price £2.50. This Portfolio was superseded by *L&NWR Non-Corridor Carriages (1886-1923)* published in 2006.

Premier Portfolio No 8 - The Holyhead Steamers of the LNWR, by A W H Pearsall & H H Davies. Published 1990, 34 pages. Cover price £3.50. A useful account of the LNWR's extensive Holyhead shipping interests.

Premier Portfolio No 9 - LNWR One Man's Passion - A tribute to G D Whitworth, edited by J Shelley. Published January 1991, 46 pages. Cover price £4.25. Dudley Whitworth was one of our founder members. The main content is a series of short essays on a variety of locomotive subjects.

Premier Portfolio No 10 - Gateway to the West - A history of Riverside Station Liverpool. MD & HB - LNWR, by Colin Reed. Published May 1992, 58 pages. Cover price £4.95. This was the first Portfolio to deal primarily with an 'infrastructure', subject. Traffic to Riverside consisted of special trains run to connect with the Trans-Atlantic liners.

Premier Portfolio No 11 - LNWR Great War Ambulance Trains, by Philip A Millard. Published May 1993, 46 pages. Cover price £6.75. It details the ambulance trains provided by the LNWR for military and navel personnel in the First World War and includes the Headquarters Staff Train.

Premier Portfolio No 12 - Recollections of Oxenholme, by W L Harris as related to Edward Talbot. Published 1994, 50 pages. Cover price £7.95. It contains observations of actual train working from 1911 giving an insight into how things were actually done. A somewhat under-rated subject.

Premier Portfolio No 13 - An Introduction to Preston, Its History, Railways and Signalling, by Richard Foster. Published 1998, 38 pages. Cover price £5.95. This publication proved popular and sold out very quickly. Copies are now very hard to find.

Premier Portfolio No 14 - The Bill Finch Portfolio, Locomotive details collected and recorded by Bill Finch. Published 1999, 58 pages. Cover price £6.95. Essential for modellers, a reprinted version is now available, titled *Building a London & North Western Railway Jumbo. The Bill Finch Portfolio of Locomotive Details.*

Premier Portfolio No 15 - London & North Western Railway Thirty Foot One Inch Carriages, by Philip A Millard. Published 2001, 45 pages. Cover price £6.95.
A new revised and much extended version of the book was produced in 2008 with 65 pages. Cover price 7.95. A large number of these carriages were built and no LNWR modeller, preservationist or historian should be without a copy!

Premier Portfolio No 16 - London & North Western Railway Company Houses, by R W Miller. Published 2004, 64 pages. Cover price 7.95. In 1921 the LNWR possessed 4325 houses and cottages for railway servants. Many of the houses were built to recognisable designs and this book describes and illustrates them. An essential guide and reference with and extensive gazetteer.

SPECIAL PUBLICATION JOINT WITH THE LANCASHIRE AND YORKSHIRE RAILWAY SOCIETY
Premier Business, compiled by Stuart Morris. A special joint publication between the London & North Western Railway Society and the Lancashire & Yorkshire Railway Society to commemorate the 150th anniversary of the formation of the LNWR. Published 1996, 50 pages.

PUBLICATIONS FROM 2005
Crewe Works Narrow Gauge System, by Edward Talbot and Clive Taylor. Published 2005, 64 pages. Cover price £8.95. This is a revised and much enlarged version of Portfolio No 5. A must for anyone interested in Crewe Works or narrow gauge railways.

L&NWR Non-Corridor Carriages, by Philip A Millard and Ian Tattersall. Published 2006, hardback 136 pages. Cover price £29.95. This was the Society's first hardback publication. It contains photographs and drawings of well over 120 types of carriages. An essential reference and no LNWR modeller, preservationist or historian should be without a copy.

The Railway Photographs of P W Pilcher, compiled by David J Patrick. Published 2007, 96 pages. Cover price £9.95. A selection of magnificent early photographs.

F W Webb 1836 - 1906, A Biography, by John E Spink. Published 2011, 96 pages. Cover price £15. An essential reference work, complementing Chacksfield's biography.

LNWR Wagons Supplement No 1, by Peter Ellis. Published 2011, 30 pages. Cover price £7.50. A supplement to the *LNWR Wagons* books covering additional vehicles.

LNWR Garston Docks, by Mike G Fell. Published 2012, 32 pages, issued in a slip case jointly with the reprint **Opening of the Stalbridge Dock Garston, February 24th 1909,** 20 pages. Combined cover price £15. Garston was the LNWR's own port.

REPRINTS
Reprint of LNWR Carriage Marshalling Circular 1910. 46 pages. First reprint June 1978. Price to members 80p, full price £1.30.

Crewe Locomotive Works - Reprinted from the original LNWR publication of 1903. 33 pages. Cover price £4.95.

LNWR Programme of the Excursion Bookings for the Summer Holidays from Euston and other London Stations 1914. 35 pages. Cover price £6.

Wolverton Carriage Works - Description of the LNWR Carriage Works at Wolverton 1906. 35 pages plus fold-out plan of the works and surrounding area.

War Record of the London & North Western Railway, by Edwin A Pratt. Published 2007, 72 pages. Cover price £8.95. It contains a wealth of information and detail on war operations on the LNWR. It is essential reading to understand the impact of the war and the contribution of the LNWR to the war effort.

LNWR Wagons, by The London & North Western Railway Society, Wild Swan Publishing.
Although not directly Society publications, this series of books is being written by a group of Society members and bear the Society's name as 'Author'. To date Volumes 1 and 2 have been published. The group consists of Mike Williams, Peter Ellis, John Shelley, Peter Davis, Tim Hughes and Bob Williams, with Chris Northedge as Editor.